ASIAN AMERICANS

RECONCEPTUALIZING CULTURE, HISTORY, POLITICS

edited by

FRANKLIN NG
CALIFORNIA STATE UNIVERSITY,
FRESNO

Asian Americans: Reconceptualizing Culture, History, Politics
Franklin Ng, series editor

BEYOND KEʻEAUMOKU

KOREANS, NATIONALISM, AND LOCAL CULTURE IN HAWAIʻI

BRENDA L. KWON

Routledge
Taylor & Francis Group

NEW YORK AND LONDON

First published 1999 by Garland Publishing, Inc.

This edition published 2013 by Routledge
711 Third Avenue, New York, NY 10017, USA
2 Park Square, Milton Park, Abingdon, Oxfordshire OX14 4RN

First issued in paperback 2016

Routledge is an imprint of the Taylor & Francis Group, an informa business

Library of Congress Cataloging-in-Publication Data

Kwon, Branda L., 1968–
    Beyond Ke'eaumoku : Koreans, nationalism, and local
culture in Hawai'i / Brenda L. Kwon.
        p.   cm. — (Asian Americans)
    Revision of the author's thesis (Ph.D.—University of Califor-
nia, Los Angeles, 1997).
    Includes bibliographical references and index.
    ISBN 0-8153-3357-9 (alk. paper)
    1. Koreans—Hawaii—History. 2. Hawaii—Ethnic relations.
3. Hawaii—Civilization. 4. Nationalism—Hawaii. I. Title.
II. Series.
DU624.7.K67K86 1999
996.9'004957—dc21
                                                        99-11031

ISBN 13: 978-1-138-96459-4 (pbk)
ISBN 13: 978-0-8153-3357-9 (hbk)

Me ke aloha pumehana
for my mother,
who never doubted me and who taught me the value of respect;
for my father,
whose importance to me grows each year;
and for my 'ohana,
who showed me how to remember where I came from.

Contents

Acknowledgments

I would like to thank the UCLA Department of English and the Institute of American Cultures for funding that aided in the completion of this project. I am also grateful to Little, Brown & Company; Gary Pak; Ty Pak; and the University of Hawai'i Press for allowing me to reprint portions of materials used here.

There are several people to whom I am indebted, and without whom this project would not have seen completion. King-Kok Cheung's care, encouragement, wisdom, and support has not only bettered my work, but has inspired me beyond my studies. I also thank Shu-mei Shih, Val Smith, and Eric Sundquist for their wonderful teaching, guidance, and insight.

During my years at UCLA, I met many people who not only challenged my thinking, but provided friendships that made Los Angeles more like home. Robert Ito has not only been a great friend and pal sympathetic to "yellow blues," but a perceptive editor and intellectual mentor. His parents, Noburo and Belle Ito, I thank for their excitement and encouragement, and for always believing in me. Karen "Kay" Wallace pushed me to keep going further in my ideas and my life; she never let me lose my perspective and, more importantly, my sense of humor. Thanks also to Mary Pat Brady for her invaluable advice and assurance; Nancy Yoo, who furnished me with sisterhood, Echowear, and endless creativity; Julie Cho, Jim Lee, Mike Murashige, Laura Pulido, and Darlene Rodrigues for being as silly and crazy as they were intelligent and thoughtful; Paula Gunn Allen, Betty Donohue, Jeanette Gilkison, and Joni Jones, for being such wonderful storytellers, companions, and morale-boosters; Carole Gentry, who never failed to share in my passions for things both in and out of academia; and those

ix

at the Academic Advancement Program, who know that teaching goes far beyond books.

Much appreciation also goes to those who inspired me to keep writing creatively, and through whom I learned I could theorize through art: Sonia Saldívar-Hull, Elaine Kim, Gary Pak, Renee Tajima-Peña, Greg Sarris, and the people at *dis.Orient Journalzine*.

At Pasadena City College, Martha Bonilla wore as many hats as she could; I wish I could express as much gratitude as is really due to her. Carrie Afuso, Milton Brown, Becky Cobb, Mel Donaldson, Nairy Finn, Robert Foreman, Diana Francisco, Harry Kawahara, Joanne Kim, Rob Lee, Susie Ling, Dona Mitoma, Roger Marheine, Dorothy Potter, Lou Rosenberg, and Beverly Tate have made PCC truly feel like a community in which I belong.

And although people will often say they learn from their students, in my case I've found that to be absolutely true. Thank you to all, especially the history-making English 52 class, who kept me focused on why I go to work each day.

After all my many years on "the mainland," the Hawai'i crowd has never stopped being as important to me as they were when we were small-kid time. The group of friends I will always think of as "the Bingham Benchies" (this includes you, Caroline) has given me such a strong sense of history and memory; I see them as the family that continues to grow with time (and weddings and babies). Thank you also to Katie Lu, whom I had the privilege to know both as a Hawai'i *and* mainland friend, for the love, trust, and intimacy she has given me; and Leslie Oyama, for all the years we took turns believing the other could do anything.

And then there is my family, who, were I to thank them as much as they deserve, would require page after page of appreciative thoughts. Dee Kuwaye, Mark Kuwaye, and Bill Kwon mean so much more than words can express—they are my anchors, my roots, *and* my friends. My grandmothers, Duk Soo Kim and Choo Soo Kwon, showed me what history really means and what it looks like. Agnes Chun helped bridge the past and the present; through her I saw the importance in giving strength to the community. Dorothy Kuwaye, Sachi Kaneshiro, and Mary and George Karatsu took me in while I was in Los Angeles, inviting me to JACCC and East West Players events, feeding me, and welcoming me into their enormous family. I am grateful that Victor Lee was always eager to help when I called to ask for Korean translations, that he always kept me informed about material on Korean Americans, and that he always offered me a place to rest. And when I think about where it all started, I know part of the blame goes to my cousins, Won Chong Kim, Mun Chilingerian, and Min Chong Kim, who nurtured my love for books and reading by catching the bus with me every Saturday to raid the Hawai'i State Library.

Most of all, thank you to my mom, Joyce Lee, for her love, spiritual guidance, and outstanding cooking, and my father, George Kwon, who, were he alive, would have been very proud.

You are all nō ka 'oi. Mahalo nui loa and kamsamnida.

About Korean, Hawaiian, and Hawai'i Creole English

This work contains many Korean and Hawaiian language terms, as well as those that are "pidgin English" or Hawai'i Creole English (HCE). I have chosen not to italicize these, or, for the most part, define them within the body of the text because these words, while they may be unfamiliar to some readers, are part and parcel of the language of the people and culture in Hawai'i and deserve to be "unmarked" as such. I have, therefore, provided a glossary at the end of the text which defines all Korean, Hawaiian, and HCE words used here. The main source of my Hawaiian definitions has been Mary Kawena Pukui and Samuel H. Elbert's *Hawaiian Dictionary: Hawaiian-English, English-Hawaiian.*

The Hawaiian language uses two diacritical marks—the macron or kahakō, and the 'okina or glottal stop—which are crucial to the understanding the meanings of these words. While "Hawai'i" is a Hawaiian language term that contains an 'okina and is spelled as such in this text, words such as "Hawaiian" or "Hawaii's" are Anglicizations, and thus I have omitted the 'okina there.

Beyond Keʻeaumoku

CHAPTER 1

The Shape of Paradise
Mapping Local Korean Territory

Literature from Hawai'i has for the most part existed as an enigma, subject to a number of misreadings by critics. At one end of the theoretical spectrum is the desire to read into island voices an expression of racial harmony and multicultural success. Stephen Sumida's argument that "American History" has painted Hawai'i as a land in which Christians sought to create the paradisiacal New World is appropriate here, since these interpretations continue to project this desire for utopia onto the islands.[1] Furthermore, scholarship that embraces this notion encourages and enforces a denial of and blindness to racial tensions in order to preserve and reify Hawaii's multicultural "specialness."

Many misreadings of Hawaii's literature have a lack of historicization at their source. This problem is certainly not new since for many people, Hawai'i exists for the pleasure of others as a playground devoid of histories. Often, when history *does* work its way into the picture, it does so via exoticism and display, functioning like a stamp in a passport that ensures one has had an "authentic" experience. Several television shows featuring special vacations in Hawai'i, for example, have operated in this manner; in one episode of the 1970's sitcom "The Brady Bunch," Bobby Brady, exploring a cave, finds a tiki that becomes a source of bad luck for the Brady family. In island lore, stories abound of those who have disturbed sacred Hawaiian sites and suffered misfortunes until the wrong was righted; these narratives succeed in calling attention to Hawaii's native origins. Yet while this particular episode of "The Brady Bunch" may indicate an awareness of

3

white intrusion on Hawaiian land under the pretext of tourism, the episode's development transforms the Bradys into saviors who foil the plans of an evil archaeologist seeking to exploit the historical site. The show ends with the triumphant Bradys at a "luau" dancing Tahitian hula with the reformed archaeologist, thus turning a cautionary tale of native violation into little more than an adventure in an exotic land.

If readings that idealize Hawai'i as a paradise are inadequate, of equal inefficacy is the impulse to critique Local literature through themes commonly found in "Asian American" literature. Because the history of Asians in Hawai'i differs from the history of Asians on the continent,[2] using continental themes results in the neglect of Hawaii's history and historical specificity. For instance, Sau-ling Wong's reading of Milton Murayama's *All I Asking For is My Body* interprets Kiyo's desire for material success in terms of a Nisei's attempt to attain the social status of haole lunas, thereby indicating his desire to be "American" or "white."[3] Yet Wong does not mention the strong Japanese influence in Hawaii's economy—a force that proved to be an obstacle to the mass interning of Hawaii's Japanese during World War II. That island Japanese have fought for and obtained a measure of collective power complicates the idea that Kiyo desires "Americanness" in the sense of social, political, and economic strength. Furthermore, as it is not uncommon for some Locals to read privilege in those of Japanese descent, one must avoid facile associations of Japaneseness with disempowerment. While Wong should be credited for including rather than marginalizing Hawaii's literature under the rubric of Asian American literature, her reading displays the problems of transplanting continental Asian American themes when interpreting Local literature.

I neither wish to endorse an insider/outsider dichotomy here, nor to assert that only those from Hawai'i should discuss Local texts. Rather, I agree with Stephen Sumida that historicizing Local literature is crucial. Reading island literature apart from its historical context isolates Hawai'i as the paradise in the middle of the sea. In order to counteract theorizing that essentializes Local culture, it is necessary to include and examine *marginalized* voices in the "paradise." Hence this project analyzes Korean American writings from Hawai'i—works that both complicate and reaffirm the position Local identity maintains in the islands. Because the first group of Koreans in Hawai'i formed a largely isolated society, their voices problematize notions of Hawaii's "specialness" by calling attention to ruptures within cherished notions of Local history, such as the belief that its origins came from plantation societies in which nonwhites unanimously banded together against haole lunas.[4] In recent years, the growing number of post-1965 immigrants in the islands has made it difficult to ignore the presence of Koreans, yet these immigrants are perceived as non-Local "outsiders" or "FOBs" with no plantation history. Contemporary cultural "space" allotted to Koreans reveals a disturbing relationship between Koreans and Local society: Korean contributions to Local culture often take the form of the appearance of kimchee on restaurant menus or, more noticeably, the proliferation of Korean bars ("KBs") in which men keep company with "hostesses." Once so concentrated on Ke'eaumoku street that "Ke'eaumoku" became synonymous with "KBs," these bars have continued to provide steady incomes for many first-generation Korean women throughout other areas of O'ahu. While it may be tempting to center this dissertation around the subordinate position of Koreans within Local culture, I find this to be less productive than examining the ways in which Korean authors from Hawai'i depict ethnic interaction in their works, which reflect particular visions of social hierarchies within island society. But the aim of this project is not to find similarities between these authors in an attempt to construct a Local Korean sensibility. Rather, I wish to show the ways in which these differing visions relate to their historical contexts. For the purpose of this discussion, I will look at three authors spanning different time periods in Hawaii's history: Margaret K. Pai, Ty Pak, and Gary Pak.

A project undertaking Korean American literature from Hawai'i faces several challenges. The relatively small number of Korean voices has made it easy for critics and historians to discount the Korean experience, which more often than not undercuts certain thematic generalizations made about Local and Asian American culture. In order to articulate some of the ways in which this exclusion occurs, I will briefly define Local identity as well as provide necessary historical background. In addition, I plan to differentiate between Local and Asian American identities, since Locals often regard "Asian American" as a continental concept. This analysis will also look at tourism and Hawaiian sovereignty, as both strongly affect constructions of Localness. Only after familiarizing ourselves with these issues can we begin to consider the political role of literature written by Koreans in Hawai'i.

LOCAL IDENTITY IN HAWAIʻI

In the wake of Hawaiian sovereignty, defining Local identity becomes a tricky task. Sovereignty groups such as Ka Lāhui Hawaiʻi and the Institute for the Advancement of Hawaiian Affairs stress the crucial differences between "Hawaiian" and "Local." In contrast to a tourist mentality that labels everything and everyone connected to the islands as "Hawaiian," and in refutation of the notion held by some Locals that one can be "Hawaiian at heart," many sovereignty groups reinforce that having indigenous Hawaiian blood is *not* the same as being "Local." "Local" can be used to refer to anyone of Asian, Hawaiian, or other Pacific Islander descent, and usually designates those who have been in Hawaiʻi for more than one generation, although more politicized definitions call for a lineage that can be traced back to the plantation labor experience. In essence, Hawaiians fall within the parameters of Local identity, though Locals are not necessarily Hawaiian. Stephen Sumida argues that whites who establish a long-term presence in the islands may be considered Local; however, it is difficult to overlook the fact that the title has largely been used to distinguish itself from "haole." During the infamous Massie trial of 1931, for instance, in which the haole wife of a naval officer accused five nonwhite men of rape, the term "Local" was first recorded as being used to racially identify the five men *as* nonwhite (two Hawaiian, two Japanese, one Chinese-Hawaiian).[5] Similarly, Ronald Takaki's overview of plantation history in Hawaiʻi calls attention to the origins of Local culture: the multiethnic makeup of the workers, intended to foment racial tension thereby preventing any solidarity among them, eventually gave rise to a Local group that separated itself from the haole lunas and plantation owners.[6]

However, Sumida rightly asserts that race is only partly at issue.[7] Localness also encompasses language, particularly Hawaiʻi Creole English (HCE), and a set of actions, behaviors, and codes prevalent in the islands, hence the term "Local-style." Another defining characteristic is a working-class background. For instance, Punahou, a prestigious private school in Hawaiʻi, was originally a missionary school for rich haole sons of missionaries and businessmen in the islands. Although with the passage of time admissions included Locals and haole women, Punahou still has retained the reputation for educating rich haole children. For many islanders,[8] then, attending the school tends to negate claims to Localness. In other words, one becomes "haolified" by virtue of the facts that one can afford to attend Punahou, and that one "speaks haole" or standard English as opposed to HCE.

Localness continues to be a specifically marked terrain that excludes in order to maintain and affirm its existence. What gets excluded often depends on whom one talks to, thus illustrating the dynamic nature of identification. For the purpose of this dissertation, I will use "Local" in two different though not unrelated capacities: the politicized definition that requires a plantation heritage, a working-class background, and a strong sense of community; and the more general definition of the community of island residents depicted by the authors as those who subscribe to a way of life most easily identifiable and representable as "Local-style," however that may be constructed in each of the authors' works.

LOCAL CULTURE AND THE RESISTANCE TO TOURISM

Those who grow up in the islands often recognize the complex nature of tourism: at the same time islanders may resent tourism for intruding upon Local lifestyles and exploiting natural resources, they understand its significance to Hawaii's economy. Since approximately 1950, tourism has been Hawaii's main commodity, following on the heels of the sandalwood, whaling, sugarcane, and pineapple industries, and the state's complicity with outside investors in grand development plans has left residents ambivalent about both government and the industry. While development destroys land and resources, and while tourism displaces Hawaii's residents in order to develop bigger resorts and golf courses, it has nevertheless become difficult to visualize alternatives. The industry does provide jobs, yet many of these jobs are in the service sector and pay well below the amount needed to reside in a place where the cost of living is among the highest in the nation.[9]

In the early 1980s, there was such antagonism toward tourism that the Hawaii Visitor's Bureau aired a commercial depicting a shriveling lei, urging residents to keep the aloha spirit, implying that Local hostility would throw Hawai'i into financial crisis.[10] This commercial confirmed the commodification of the aloha spirit, blurring the line between a way of life and the need to sell oneself for the sake of the island's economic survival. A decade later, the resistance to tourism has not diminished. The prevailing notion of Waikīkī as an overpriced, plastic landscape reflects the continuing desire to draw distinctions between it and the "real" O'ahu; yet in making these distinctions, residents may unwittingly internalize ideas of the "real" Hawai'i as both a geographical and racial paradise. Recent developments in the movements for Hawaiian sovereignty, for instance, necessitate reevaluations of history and the position of native Hawaiians within Local arenas, yet the denial of and even hostility towards the more outspoken voices within the movements demonstrates how strongly some residents feel about protecting their vision of Hawai'i. The danger thus lies in the potential for Local culture's opposition to tourism to romanticize the islands. With regards to cultural production, much may be omitted for the sake of maintaining and authenticating that ideal vision. Perhaps not so ironically, all of this works to strengthen and reaffirm the power of the tourist industry. At the same time that Local culture resists Waikīkī and tourism, it creates an authenticity that tourism ultimately accesses and commodifies. For example, one can purchase any number of Local Motion or Town and Country[11] products in the Ala Moana/Waikiki areas as souvenirs that represent the "Hawaiian experience" more enticingly than a plastic lei.

To counter tourism's appropriation of Local culture, we must examine the ruptures, inconsistencies, and contradictions within Localness in order to more fully understand and affirm it, and to provide a larger base upon which resistance can be built. The impulse to do exactly this could be seen in the 1970s literary renaissance in which Local writers and artists contested dominant images of the islands as a tourist playground. By initiating the rebirth of cultural histories, they took issue with an idyllic paradise that "denies history."[12] The emphasis here on diversity indicated the need for various voices to provide a complex historical presence where one had been denied.

Yet it is my contention that this diversity nonetheless resulted in the marginalization of voices such as those of Korean Americans in the islands, in part because they don't quite "fit." Three factors account for their erasure in this respect. First, Korea's political history with Japan influenced the isolationism of Koreans in Hawai'i and encouraged a division between "Local" and "Korean," especially since Koreans sought to differentiate themselves from other ethnic groups, namely the Japanese. Next, as the second generation of Koreans outmarried at a high rate, seemingly implying an integration of Koreans into Local society, Korean identities became subsumed by Local ones. Third, the large numbers of post-1965 Korean immigrants lent credibility to the perception of island Koreans as monolithically "FOB," with no Local history.[13] Together, these conditions made it relatively easy to render Koreans in Hawai'i invisible, as outsiders to Local society. This overlooking ultimately enables tourism to continue to colonize, for if the act of colonization relies upon the reduction of the Other, then it follows that the obverse—complicating the Other—provides a valuable means of resistance.

If island residents live in a system that actively accesses, consumes, and commodifies the "authenthic," however, where does "authentic resistance" exist? Because tourism has been the mainstay of Hawaii's economy, preservation and commodification have become intertwined. Thus tourist interest determines the value of Hawaiian historical and cultural sites, regardless of their value to native Hawaiians. Pali Lookout will never become luxury housing, despite its breathtaking view of Windward Oahu, because of its tourist appeal as the location at which Kamehameha the First drove his enemies off the cliff. In contrast, sacred nohaku hānau[14] in Aiea are imprisoned within graffiti-marked cement walls and behind iron bars just outside a residential front yard. Tourism designs a map in which certain historical sites claim more importance than others, and the creation of these sellable points of interest works in such a way that island residents value these places at the same time they avoid them for being too "touristy." In other words, Locals experience the impulse to both value and reject tourist geography while seeking to establish their own cultural space.

The struggles over "authentic" landmarks once again reflects the battle between residents who wish to claim the space of "real Hawai'i" and the tourist industry that wants to find and exploit this "realness." Further complicating this is the fact that like Locals, tourism wishes to keep the lines between "native" and "visitor" distinct, although those lines are drawn according to very different criteria. As Edward Said points out, the dominant culture's distinctions between "us" and "them" are entirely "arbitrary," as the dominant culture believes that "[i]t is enough for 'us' to set up these boundaries in our own minds; 'they' become 'they' accordingly, and both their territory and their mentality are designated as different from 'ours.'"[15]

Louis Adrian Montrose's anecdote about sixteenth-century Amazons exemplifies what happens to the Other's land as conquest ensues. If, as he points out, Amazons were always relocated "just within the receding boundary of terra incognita,"[16] then as "our" knowledge of the world's geography grows, the land of the Other disappears. Yet it does *not* disappear. In the case of the tourist industry, investors and developers simply rewrite "terra cognita" into desirable and undesirable space, relegating the Other to undesirable territory. The attempted eviction of Waiāhole-Waikāne residents in the 1970s to build luxury condominiums, as well as the development of Local recreation spots such as Point Panic and Kewalo Basin, attest to the systematic removal of Local bodies from valued property. Furthermore, the heavy population of ʻAʻala Park, a longtime homeless haven with roots dating back the early plantation labor strikes in the 1920s,[17] bore witness to Locals who found themselves pushed out of the tourist landscape.

The need for containment and control lies at the crux of this kind of rescripting of terra cognita. During the Los Angeles Riots,[18] for instance, the area perceived as "South Central" by the media began to expand its borders as the fires and looting spread toward the La Cienega area.[19] Designating this area as "South Central" operated in such a way that the privileged could ask, "Why are *they* destroying *their own* communities?" When the threat approached Beverly Hills and the Westside, however, residents of those areas armed themselves and literally defended the borders. It became clear that the areas that were surrendered to "South Central" stood apart from what was considered by the privileged to be the inviolable "us."

Local geography resists a tourist industry that seeks to push Locals outside of the "inviolable us"; in order to maintain an oppositional stance, Locals need territory outside of the tourist map. The increasing need for Local surfers to "go country"—that is, to surf the North Shore—is one instance of this phenomenon.[20] Yet in this particular battle over borders, Local culture and tourism desire power over each other and in fact define and depend upon each other. Although Local literature combats essentializing by presenting complexity and diversity, it also stops short of an inclusivity that threatens to deconstruct the concepts of "Localism." What results is similar to the reification of U.S. nationalism that certain Asian American critics, in search of "Asian America," have advocated in the past:

In urging the formation of a strategic essentialist Asian American cultural nationalism unified under U.S. history, many Asian American critics ironically repeat the call of U.S. nationalists for a shared unified American identity in response to the threat of fragmentation posed by minority interest groups.[21]

Hence certain "disruptive" voices are sacrificed in the name of unity. This places a certain burden, then, on a study such as the one I undertake here, in that the kind of questions I wish to ask may be perceived as traitorous. Yet this is exactly my point—that through such a threat of exclusion and disownment by Local culture, challenges fall by the wayside and Localness remains intact in its principles and in its systems of legitimization.

LOCALS, ASIAN AMERICANS, AND KOREAN PLANTATION HISTORY

During the 1993 "Strategizing Cultures" conference held at UCLA, University of Hawai'i professor Ricardo J. Trimillo launched a discussion of identity within the Asian American community with an anecdote. Trimillo and a colleague were on a plane bound for Los Angeles, and upon arrival at LAX, Trimillo's colleague turned to him and said, "Well, we're Asian Americans now."[22] This comment illustrated that the distance between Hawai'i and the continent extended beyond the geographical, and that Localness saw itself apart from Asian Americanness.[23]

In the 1970s, a group of outspoken writers including Frank Chin and Jeffrey Paul Chan sought to politicize and define an Asian American identity, asserting in their introduction to the anthology *Aiiieeeee!* that

> Seven generations of suppression under legislative racism and euphemized white racist love have left today's Asian-Americans in a state of self-contempt, self-rejection, and disintegration. We have been encouraged to believe that we have no cultural integrity as Chinese- or Japanese-Americans, that we are either Asian (Chinese or Japanese) or American (white), or are measurably both. This myth of being either/or and the equally goofy concept of the dual personality haunted our lobes while our rejection by both Asian and white

America proved we were neither one nor the other. Nor were we half
and half or more one than the other. . . . The age, variety, depth and
quality of the writing collected here proves the existence of Asian-
American sensibilities and cultures *that might be related to but are
distinct from Asia and white America.*[24]

Here, the authors claim both Asianness and Americanness as a
birthright, although they reject both in favor of a separate identity. This
move points to contradictory impulses to attach roots to both
homelands, yet reject the consequences of those roots, thus positing a
hybridity that is not hybrid. While excerpts from works such as John
Okada's *No-No Boy* and Carlos Bulosan's *America is in the Heart*
included in the anthology problematize Americanness, they nevertheless
affirm that the protagonists are as unquestionably "American" as anyone
else. That this "Americanness" is based on constructions of whiteness,
however, undermines the primary agenda of establishing a distinct
identity. Instead of resisting hegemonic notions of nationality in this
case, such works as Okada's and Bulosan's ultimately embrace them.[25]

In contrast, Local literature focuses less on proving Americanness
than on capturing the dynamics of Hawaii's communities.[26] Many
Locals readily claim an American affiliation, so much so that the topic
rarely arises. When asked about race or ethnicity, Locals generally do
not identify for instance as "Filipino American" or "Korean American,"
but simply as "Filipino" or "Korean," since American nationality is
already assumed. Americanness in Hawai'i usually becomes
questionable only in the case of "FOBs," although foreignness in the
islands can describe both haoles and "FOBs." The presence of "katonks"
further complicates this system of classification.[27] In a place where
Asians describe themselves as "Orientals," the term "Asian American"
commonly operates as a "katonk" term, reinforcing the notion that
Asian Americans have had to see their Americanness as doubtful. One
begins to discern, then, a connection between the dismissal of
"katonks" and the marginalization of Koreans in Hawai'i. Two
questions arise that I will attempt to answer in subsequent chapters: If
asserting Americanness is identified as a "katonk" rather than a Local
agenda, what role does Korean nationalism play in the marginalization
of Koreans in Hawai'i, given that Korean oppression under Japanese
rule gave rise to a view of westernization and Americanization as
messianic and desirable? Furthermore, how does the post-1965 group of

immigrants to Hawai'i, largely perceived as "FOB," hence "Asian" in culture and influence, add to their construction as "foreigners" to the islands?

Having done research on Local history, I often found myself frustrated by certain assumptions about Local culture that the history of Koreans in Hawai'i easily challenges. The year 2003 marks the 100th anniversary of the arrival of the first large group of Koreans in the islands; prior to that date, small numbers immigrated to the states mainly to pursue educations and escape political persecution by the Japanese. A little under 100 years later, Korean history in America is still largely unknown; more dismaying is the fact that sources choosing to discuss it often misrepresent the position of early Koreans. For example, the account in *Strangers From a Different Shore* of the 1920 Japanese and Filipino workers' plantation labor strike, often deemed the first multiethnic strike in Hawai'i, glosses over Korean strikebreaking with disturbing implications:

> To break the strike directly, planters enlisted Hawaiians, Portuguese, and Koreans as strikebreakers. They knew that Koreans had a particular enmity for the Japanese, and the planters had consistently used Koreans to help break Japanese strikes. During the 1920 strike, Korean laborers under the leadership of the Korean National Association announced: "We place ourselves irrevocably against the Japanese and the present strike. We don't wish to be looked upon as strikebreakers, but we shall continue to work . . . and we are opposed to the Japanese in everything." More than one hundred Korean men and women organized themselves into a Strikebreakers' Association and offered their services to the Hawaiian Sugar Planters' Association. . . . Though they had been soundly beaten, the workers had learned a valuable lesson from the 1920 strike. Filipinos and Japanese, joined by Spanish, Portuguese, and Chinese laborers, had participated in the first major interethnic working-class struggle in Hawaii.[28]

The language Takaki uses here depicts Koreans as instigating Korean-Japanese tensions, and in failing to elaborate upon Hawaiian and Portuguese participation in strikebreaking, he constructs Koreans as the leading adversaries to what is later hailed as a triumphant multiethnic movement. Furthermore, Takaki's account leaves the reader with only vague notions at best of Japanese colonization, because he neglects to elucidate Korean "enmity."[29] For instance, the author's omission of the landmark 1919 Mansei Rebellion in Korea erases this event and decontextualizes Korean strikebreaking in Hawaiʻi.[30] Dismissed in this narrative, Japan's one hundred-year assault in fact cannot be separated from Koreans' presence in the United States, their animosity towards Japanese in Hawaiʻi, and their exclusion from Local culture.

Wilma Sur elaborates upon these issues by delineating the ways in which Koreans saw America and westernization as the key to Korea's liberation, despite the U.S.'s history of ignoring their cries for help.[31] Once in the islands, Koreans felt that their successful assimilation would gain American support: if they could prove themselves good and loyal citizens, then Americans would be more sympathetic to the plight in Korea. Assimilation, then, meant refusal to strike as well as separation from other Local groups. Koreans in Hawaiʻi, then, found themselves in the precarious situation of living in exile while seeking to liberate Korea, and establishing a new home in a foreign land. These impulses conflicted with each other in regards to social interaction and contributed to the exclusion of Koreans, which undercuts the perception of Local culture as a multicultural society that "enhances interethnic cooperation instead of internecine rivalry."[32]

Two major influences commonly regarded as the roots of Hawaii's multicultural "unity" are the plantation societies and the International Longshoremen's and Warehousemen's Union (ILWU). David E. Thompson, referring to the 1920 Japanese and Filipino laborers' strike in his assessment of the ILWU as "a force for interracial unity," notes that the ILWU helped to foster and continue what had been a growing interracial unification among different groups on the plantations. While Thompson discusses the difficulties with ethnic conflict that occurred during the union's formation, he omits any discussion of Korean participation. Whether this results from the relatively small number of Koreans in the islands or from deliberate erasure, the fact remains that Korean nationalist agendas and resentment of Japanese in Hawaiʻi would have undercut the force of his assertion that the ILWU harmonized a racially divided society.

By bringing workers of all races together for a common effort, by providing them with many shared experiences, by providing a consistent, logical, and practical pressure against exclusive habits and the expression of prejudice, by a similar pressure toward the establishment of issues rather than labels or "personalities" as the criterion of judgment, the ILWU has done much to remove racial tension and promote interracial aloha and unity among its members.[33]

The point here is not to deny that the ILWU had a tremendous effect on the Hawaii's multiculturalism. Simply put, it would appear that union politics becomes yet another vehicle for the reinscription of paradise that comes at the expense of Local Korean history.

THE COLORS OF EXILE: KOREAN AMERICAN WRITERS FROM HAWAI'I

With Local literature and Korean American literature emerging as relatively new fields of study, the intersection of the two yields a small number of authors whose works this dissertation will analyze. What I wish to do here is to briefly rearticulate issues I have raised in this introduction through the works of three Korean American writers from Hawai'i: Margaret K. Pai, Ty Pak, and Gary Pak.

At once a celebration and critique of the American Dream, Margaret K. Pai's *The Dreams of Two Yi-Min* illustrates the interplay between Americanness, Local identity, and Korean nationalism. Demonstrating the impact capitalism and geography have on race, gender, nationalism, and nationality, the narrative depicts the Kwon family's search for arrival within both Local and continental contexts. Americanness, represented by the attainment of wealth and stability in the U.S., demands that the family erase their Korean affiliations in a variety of ways that prove to be geographically specific: what works for them in the islands fails in California, in part because their racial identities change, thus necessitating a renegotiation of sacrifices. While geography influences concepts of "American," "Korean," and "Local," class status also comes into play. The loss of class privilege for the protagonist's mother Hee Kyung in the move from Korea to the U.S. prompts her passion for Korean nationalism, because it reinstates her yangban (upperclass) consciousness. In contrast, her husband Do In's laborer background causes him to embrace the American Dream ideology that offers him economic mobility. The couple's varying relationships to Korean nationalism in turn affect their gender roles as they struggle to maintain a traditional familial structure. Much more than an "immigrant success story," Pai's work reveals that nationality is never an unrelated, isolated, or ahistorical construct. Largely taking as its subject the lives of post-1965 Korean immigrants to the U.S., Ty Pak's work emphasizes the importance of adopting a transnational perspective in reading nationality. Korea and its memories inform many of the characters' identities on the continent and in Hawai'i, underscoring the need for a global perspective in defining such concepts as "Korean American" and "Local." While in Pak's stories it is clear that "American" becomes dependent upon "Korean," the emphasis on exile points to his protagonists' inability to claim either lands or cultures for varying historical reasons. The slipperiness of identity recurs throughout the collection, as does the use of women as vehicles of border-crossing. Depicting the tension between historical memory and adopting a new land that requires the erasure of this memory, *Guilt Payment* illuminates the impact of post-1965 immigrants' experiences upon the conception of Koreans as outsiders to Local culture.

Finally, Gary Pak's *The Watcher of Waipuna and Other Stories* focuses on social relationships within Hawaii's Local communities and takes issue with tourism and the impulse to dehistoricize the islands' rich and complex past. Land issues lie at the crux of many of Pak's stories, as questions of ownership in the battle between Hawaiians, Locals, and multinational corporations become rooted deep within the 'āina. Pak presents his readers with stories in which various histories collide and push consciously against touristic notions of an unremittingly peaceful Hawai'i. Pak's novel, *A Ricepaper Airplane*, interrogates dominant narratives of Hawaii's Local history. By fusing together the histories of Local culture and Korean nationalism in Hawai'i, Pak creates and enforces a space for a specifically *Local Korean* history. Such a move becomes both complex and subversive, in that *A Ricepaper Airplane* calls for an inclusivity that radically ruptures prevailing notions of Localness, and reclaims a heretofore overlooked position for Local Koreans.

Together, these authors and texts create a collective voice and history that at the very least demands dialogue.

The main vehicle of my interrogation and exploration of Local culture is literature, more specifically, the close-reading of texts written by Koreans from Hawai'i. While I feel that literary studies have moved more and more towards "critical theory," I have chosen not to follow this route, particularly because I see within it a potentially dangerous tendency to reestablish first and third world constructions where theory-oriented arguments are seen as more "sophisticated" or academically "valuable" than close-readings. This position assumes that what writers and close-readers do is *not* theoretical, and threatens to turn the study of literature into an increasingly exclusive practice. Furthermore, I do not wish to write about hierarchies and systems of exclusion by using methods that may replicate those practices. I do not question the value of literary and critical theory here, only its privileged position. Of course, the very fact that I am undertaking this project for a major research university already puts me in a privileged position, and I have had to contend with my own questioning of my motives for writing about this particular subject.

Admittedly, my choice of authors is governed in part by the availability of their work; certainly, I might have researched plantation and church publications, or student journals, or poems written by Koreans in their native language. Two main factors have shaped the course of my analysis: my inability to read, write, or speak Korean; and my interest in the material that has been legitimized for consumption by what might be called authoritative Local publishers. Because I wish to interrogate the position of Koreans in Local culture and consciousness, my interest is in a kind of "mainstream" authoring that reflects a high point of negotiation between "personal vision" and public acceptability. My selection of texts privileges English-speaking and writing authors who have been able to maintain some kind of foothold within Local arenas, rather than those Koreans perhaps most marginalized in Hawai'i—poor immigrants. Yet I hope this project begins to explain the marginalization of those who have not been able to express their visions through such avenues as literary publication. I see what I have done here as a starting point only, and it is my wish that more scholarship will take as its subject the cultural sites I have not covered in this work.

NOTES

1. See Stephen Sumida, "Sense of Place, History, and the Concept of the 'Local' in Hawaii's Asian/Pacific American Literatures," in *Reading the*

Literatures of Asian America, ed. Shirley Geok-lin Lim and Amy Ling (Philadelphia: Temple University Press, 1992), 215-238.

2. In keeping with recent scholarship on the subject of Hawaiʻi, I use the term "continent" here as opposed to "mainland," as the latter term tends to establish a dominant-subordinate relationship between the continental U.S. and Hawaiʻi.

3. See Sau-ling Cynthia Wong, *Reading Asian American Literature: From Necessity to Extravagance* (Princeton: Princeton University Press, 1993), 47.

4. Korean immigration to Hawaiʻi falls into two main eras: 1903-1924, and post-1965. A number of factors explain this hiatus, the most significant being the enactment of the Oriental Exclusion Act of 1924 that barred Asian immigration to the U.S. Subsequent chapters will deal with the heterogeneity of Koreans in Hawaiʻi. For the purpose of this chapter, I will highlight as my scope the initial group of first-generation laborers that separated themselves from other ethnicities in the islands during a period that is commonly perceived to have given birth to Local society.

5. Eric Yamamoto, "From 'Japanee' to Local: Community Change and the Redefinition of Sansei Identity in Hawaii" (master's thesis, University of Hawaiʻi, 1974), 105.

6. Ronald Takaki, *Pau Hana: Plantation Life and Labor in Hawaii* (Honolulu: University of Hawaiʻi Press, 1983).

7. Stephen Sumida, *And the View from the Shore: Literary Traditions of Hawaiʻi* (Seattle: University of Washington Press, 1991), xiv-xv.

8. I use the term "islanders" here and "residents" elsewhere, as opposed to "Locals," since the latter is a loaded and much contested term.

9. See Leroy O. Laney, "'Why Is the Cost of Living In Hawaii So High? Will It Ever Come Down?,'" in *The Price of Paradise: Lucky We Live Hawaii?*, ed. Randall W. Roth (Honolulu: Mutual, 1992), 23-31.

10. I thank Robert Ito for calling my attention to this commercial.

11. Both are popular brands of surf equipment and clothing worn by Locals.

12. Sumida, "Sense of Place," 215.

13. Between the period of 1924-1965, some Koreans did immigrate to the U.S. as families of U.S. military servicemen, and as adopted children. However, the relatively small number of these immigrants in comparison to the post-1965 group causes their erasure in Local consciousness. Although the writers I intend to examine do not fall into this group, mention is made

of servicemen's wives and children in Ty Pak's *Guilt Payment*, and it is these images that I will explore in this project.

14. To ensure that their children would possess extra power, ali'i women would give birth upon designated sacred stones. The power of these stones was such that if a common woman could access and bear her children on these stones, her offspring would be considered ali'i. See Scott Cunningham, *Hawaiian Religion & Magic* (St. Paul, MN: Llewellyn, 1995), 104-105.

15. Edward W. Said, *Orientalism* (New York: Vintage, 1978), 54.

16. Louis Adrian Montrose, "A Midsummer Night's Dream and the Shaping Fantasies of Elizabethan Culture: Gender, Power, Form," in *Rewriting the Renaissance*, ed. Margaret W. Ferguson, Maureen Quilligan, and Nancy J. Vickers (Chicago: Chicago University Press, 1986), 71.

17. The recent decision to evict the homeless from both 'A'ala Park and Sand Island demonstrates another rewriting of terra cognita. Both house many Hawaiian residents, who constitute the largest ethnic percentage of homeless. It is interesting that this eviction came at roughly the same time that Hawaiian sovereignty movements were gaining momentum.

18. I use the word "riots" here carefully. While I do agree that the fires and looting that took place after the LAPD verdict came as a result of years of political and economic oppression, I also feel that the Korean American community was scapegoated in much of the violence.

19. I thank Kevin Frank for pointing this out.

20. While "in-town" spots like Ala Moana and Point Panic still remain favorites with Local surfers, tourists have decreased the attractiveness of these places. I thank Craig Hirai for his help with this example.

21. Shirley Geok-lin Lim, "Immigration and Diaspora," in *An Interethnic Companion to Asian American Literature*, ed. King-Kok Cheung (New York: Cambridge University Press, 1997), 291.

22. Ricardo J. Trimillo, (panel discussion at the "Strategizing Cultures" conference sponsored by the University of California at Los Angeles, Spring 1993).

23. See Jonathan Y. Okamura, "Why There Are no Asian Americans in Hawai'i: The Continuing Significance of Local Identity," *Social Process in Hawaii* 35 (1994): 161-178.

24. Frank Chin et al., eds., *Aiiieeeee!: An Anthology of Asian-American Writers* (Washington, D.C.: Howard University Press, 1983), viii, my emphasis.

25. Stephen Sumida likewise argues that a great deal of Asian American literature, in positioning itself against "America," reifies "racial, cultural, and national constructs of a perceived 'majority' American culture." He also contends that the "America" desired in such works as Bulosan's and Okada's is an idealized and inclusive America, rather than one that deals with Asian American participation in a nation that continues to colonize native peoples. See Stephen Sumida, "Postcolonialism, Nationalism, and the Emergence of Asian/Pacific American Literatures," in *An Interethnic Companion to Asian American Literature*, ed. King-Kok Cheung (New York: Cambridge University Press, 1997), 274-288.

26. Although Jon Shirota's *Lucky Come Hawaii* does question national claims, it significantly takes place within the landscape of World War II Hawaiʻi after the bombing of Pearl Harbor, when Japanese in the islands were perceived as "dangerous" and the U.S. made interrogations of national affiliations its primary concern.

27. Stephen Sumida and Gary Okihiro both define "katonk" specifically as a Japanese American from the continent, but the term has expanded somewhat to refer to any Asian American raised on the continent. See Stephen Sumida, *And the View from the Shore*, xvi, and Gary Okihiro, "The Picnic," *Japanese American National Museum Quarterly* 10.2 (1995): 4-11.

28. Ronald Takaki, *Strangers From a Different Shore* (New York: Penguin, 1989), 153-154.

29. Texts such as Theresa Cha's *Dictee*, Kyung Soo Cha's *Pumpkin Flower & Patriotism*, and Sook Nyul Choi's *Year of Impossible Goodbyes* are important precisely because they *do* elaborate upon the horrors of the occupation that the Japanese government still refuses to admit.

30. I thank King-Kok Cheung for this astute observation.

31. In the Taft-Katsura Agreement of 1905 following Japan's victory in the Russo-Japanese War, the U.S. agreed not to interfere in Japan's colonization of Korea in exchange for Japan's acquiescence in the U.S.'s rule over the Philippines. Similarly, following World War I, President Wilson refused to meet with a group of Korean delegates seeking independence, and a petition for independence was rebuffed at the Paris Peace conference because of Japan's strong objections. Ironically, Wilson's "Fourteen Points," the doctrine of Self-Determination, served as a major inspiration to and guiding force for Korean nationalism. See Sucheng Chan, introduction to *Quiet Odyssey: A Pioneer Korean Woman in America*, by Mary Paik Lee, ed. Sucheng Chan (Seattle: University of Washington Press, 1990), xviii, xxix.

32. See Glen Grant and Dennis M. Ogawa, "Living Proof: Is Hawaii the Answer?", *ANNALS, AAPSS* 530 (November 1993): 137-154.

33. David E. Thompson, "The ILWU as a Force for Interracial Unity in Hawaii," in *Kodomo No Tame Ni: The Japanese American Experience in Hawaii*, ed. Dennis M. Ogawa and Glen Grant (Honolulu: University of Hawai'i Press, 1978), 508.

CHAPTER 2

The Myth of the American Dream
Margaret K. Pai's *The Dreams of Two Yi-Min*

When I was in the first grade, a photographer came to my elementary school to take pictures of the students. He wanted ethnically diverse children for a poster whose purpose and organization I now have forgotten. He only needed a small group—we ran screaming to our teachers, hands waving frantically in the air, shrieking "Me! Me!" Our teachers thought that, to be fair, we should rotate groups for each shot. *Shea, Roxanne, Joseph, Claudia.* They explained that we couldn't all be in the pictures. *Matthew, Julie, Debbie, Kehau.* We took our chances, though. *Kerry, Wendy, Craig, Debra.* I raised my hand every time, like all the other first graders. *Kent, Alapaki, Sharolyn, Vance.* And they chose me for every picture.

I knew they picked me because I was Korean. As one of the few Koreans at my school, and the only one in my grade, I was *special.* In fact, I remained special until the third grade when Mi Young walked into our classroom. A haole family had adopted her from Korea, and she couldn't speak English. That entire year, our teachers made us partners because of our "sameness." I tried to befriend her, though I could only utter some numbers and food words in hangul. Everyone said she was an FOB from Korea. I couldn't explain my difference from her, but in my six year-old head, I knew her kind of Korean and my kind of Korean were worlds apart.

To everyone else, we were foreigners. No one really knew what to do with Koreans; they thought that a lot of the Koreans around were FOBs, or bar girls working the Ke'eaumoku strip. But that was it. The lyrics of a song I used to hear, "Mr. Sun Cho Lee," made fun of stingy old Chinese, Japanese, Filipino, and Hawaiian men—even a Hawaiian woman. But there were no Koreans. We didn't really exist in island culture. Until my teenage years, I didn't even know Koreans worked on the plantations. I happened to ask about my grandfather one day, and I remember feeling surprised that one side of our family had been in Hawaiʻi that long. Even now, if people ask me when my family came to the islands, I take care to mention my father's family, who worked in the fields of Waialua.

The *strangeness* of Koreans and their general exclusion from Local culture in island consciousness bears examination not only for its historical value, but because of its continuing social effects. As many Koreans have been long-time residents of Hawaiʻi with roots in the plantations, it seems appropriate to begin with Margaret K. Pai's *The Dreams of Two Yi-Min*, which details the struggles of two such Koreans, Do In and his wife Hee Kyung. Although Koreans do have a shared history of plantation labor with other races in Hawaiʻi, the impact of Korea's political situation abroad on Koreans in Hawaiʻi has made it difficult to access this history and the legitimization that comes with it. In this chapter, I will examine how political relationships between Korea, Japan, and the U.S. play out in the Kwon family's establishment in Hawaiʻi, namely through three themes: 1) the instability of first and third world boundaries in Do In's and Hee Kyung's move to Hawaiʻi; 2) the collapse of home and work spaces in their pursuit of economic stability, as well as the effects of this collapse on gender and national identity; and 3) the failure of narratives established for the Kwons in Hawaiʻi to translate to and exist on the continental U.S. The aim here is not to determine when and if the Kwons can identify as Locals, but to focus on the issues that inform and construct the experiences of the Kwons. This will lead us to reexamine certain long-held notions of Local culture, as well as illuminate the hierarchies that exist within it.

Cane

On our drive to Kuilima
we pass fields of cane,
tall and sturdy, shifting in the breeze,
lovely hula hands
beckoning us to wander

among their razor-sharp shoots.
The rows of green promise
sweetness, Old Hawai'i,
but history and the six-o-clock news
have taught us different.
In the fields lay missing persons,
recovered too late—
we learned early to hear ghosts
rustling deep among the stalks,
and we wondered as police
moved like workers in lines, searching,
if they too heard ghosts,
shaking cane in their anger.

Driving inland to Haleiwa
I imagine roads you came to hate,
under a sun that burned the paper
of your already brown skin.
For you these fields meant
weary hands and a broken back,
laying track after track for a train
you'd never ride.
How many times did you dream of home
before digging up the picture
you kept of your youth,
to be creased and fluttering
in the hands of a bride?
And when she came to you
did you understand
this white horse woman,
who made it your destiny
never to tame her?

Harabuji,
you would never see my face,
though I would later trace
letters of your name
carved in weathered grey marble.
Deep into Waialua

is your weary gift to me—
the sight of these green fields
with longing and sadness;
this inheritance built and wrought
from the labor of your years
as if one day to say look
to the child whose face presses on the window.

Although the first large group of Korean immigrants to Hawai'i arrived in 1903, between 1896 and 1902 a small number of Korean students and diplomats came to the islands, many of them en route to the continental U.S. While 1903 appears "late" compared to the arrival of Chinese and Japanese laborers in the 1850s and 1880s respectively, this date is significant for two reasons. Although Japan did not officially annex Korea until 1910, it had forcefully attempted colonization of the peninsula since the mid-nineteenth century. Among those who immigrated to the U.S. prior to 1903, then, were Korean patriots seeking the help of the U.S. government in maintaining their country's independence. Japanese aggression and terrorism meanwhile grew increasingly oppressive, and in the years surrounding the annexation, many Koreans left the homeland in order to escape.[1]

Second, with the effect of the Chinese Exclusion Act in 1882 that prohibited the entry of Chinese to the U.S., plantation owners in Hawai'i faced a depletion of cheap labor. For the most part, the success they had had with Chinese and Japanese labor diminished their need for other workers, as the owners were able to pit the groups against each other, thereby preventing any worker solidarity that might threaten the plantation structure.[2] Faced with a loss of Chinese labor and unwilling to import expensive European labor, the Hawaiian Sugar Planters' Association (HSPA)[3] made plans to offset the power of the Japanese majority by recruiting Koreans, whom they perceived as ideal workers:

> I feel as confident as I can without positively knowing, that the Koreans will prove good laborers if we can get them to the Islands. . . . [The Koreans] are lusty strong fellows and physically much the superior of the Japs. . . . [I]n rice culture and mining work they excel any other nationality.[4]

In addition, the planters, who were well aware of the deterioration of the Yi dynasty under Japanese rule, used Korea's political climate to further their objectives:

> I feel . . . that as compared with the Japs [Koreans] will be more permanent as they should have no home ties or at least should have none considering the way they are ground down at home, and the advantages they would enjoy in the Islands as compared with what they have at home should tend to make them a fixture [in Hawai'i].[5]

The planters originally proposed the "Korean solution" in 1896, redrafting plans in 1898 and 1901 in order to circumvent a number of obstacles, including the outlawing of contract labor in the U.S. and the Japanese presence in Korea.[6] Beginning in 1902, then, the HSPA began active recruitment.[7]

Eager to secure Korean contract labor, the plantation owners solicited Koreans by encouraging them to settle and establish families in Hawai'i; importing women thus became an important item on their agenda. Nearly ten percent of the 6,685 Koreans who entered Hawai'i between 1903 and 1906 were women, and by 1920, Korean women constituted 21 percent of the Korean adult immigrant population in the U.S.[8] However, like Chinese, Japanese, and Filipino plantation societies, Korean society in Hawai'i consisted mainly of bachelors.[9] In efforts to remedy the problem and prevent unrest among the workers that might jeopardize sugar production, the HSPA decided to import brides from Korea, especially since most Korean laborers refused matches with non-Korean women in Hawai'i. Consequently, between 1912 and 1924, many of those leaving Korea were picture brides seeking opportunities in America and liberation from poor living conditions under the Japanese.

As with other immigrants, the dream of America as a land of wealth and freedom seduced these picture brides. The strong Western Christian influence in Korea that allowed Korean women a relatively large measure of mobility in a repressive Confucian society reinforced this vision: as Christians, Korean women found they could socialize with others and attend functions such as church services outside the home. Furthermore, during a time in which the Japanese discouraged and later prohibited Korean culture and language, Christianity provided a

safe site of resistance for Koreans.[10] Hence America and the West soon
came to equal sanctuary as well as political and economic freedom:

> My parents were very poor. One year, a heavy rain came, a flood;
> the crops all washed down. Oh, it was a very hard time, you
> know. . . . Under the Japanese, no freedom. Not even free
> talking. My auntie told me that my cousin was living where
> picture brides come, Hawaii. . . . Hawaii's a free place,
> everybody living well. Hawaii had freedom, so if you like talk,
> you can talk; you like work, you can work. I wanted to come, so, I
> sent my picture.[11]

Yet this freedom would prove illusory, and the crossing of borders
would involve deception. Because photos were a luxury item, most men
sent pictures they kept of themselves as young men; consequently,
many brides discovered themselves marrying men significantly older
than their pictures revealed: "'When I first saw my fiancé, I could not
believe my eyes,' said Anna Choi, who was fifteen years old when she
became a picture bride. 'His hair was grey and I could not see any
resemblances to the picture I had. He was forty-six years old.'"[12]

To entice brides, the men also exaggerated their wealth and status,
when in reality they were poor laborers. For many picture brides,
distinctions between "third world" Korea and "first world" U.S. broke
down as they encountered struggle, poverty, and oppression in their new
homes. Many of the women ultimately worked alongside their husbands
in the plantations, or ran boarding houses in which they would care for
the other Korean laborers, in efforts to survive in Hawai'i.

Margaret K. Pai's memoir *The Dreams of Two Yi-Min* begins in
this particular era. The title evokes the American Dream as well as its
guarantee of success with hard work, yet the novel reveals the
complexity of such a promise. Hee Kyung's and her husband Do In's
efforts to attain their dreams both dismantle and reify class, gender, and
racial borders as the family negotiates its role as part of the "small
minority among the races in Hawaii." That is, because Hee Kyung
comes from a yangban background and Do In, a farmer's, their readings
of financial success and hardship vary dramatically. The family also
contends with shifting racializations and gender roles which cause them
to reconstruct their identities, as Local and continental geographies

define borders in distinct and separate ways, thus illustrating the dynamic nature of the myth of the American Dream.

White Horse Woman

*The moment you snatch the picture
from her hand, her eyes widen
with understanding and implication.
To appease her you trade husbands,
give her the young, educated man
in exchange for the old, dark worker
waiting expectantly on the dock.
To you this twist of fate
meant less than preserving appearances—
a young girl's hysteria brought
jeopardy for the rest,
and what you do is less from love or care
than shrewdness and the understanding
of what it means to survive.
Over the years you both
bear three sons and a daughter,
as if to remind you of your tampering—
and as she caresses the cheek of
your daughter, my aunt,
she whispers over and over*
I should have been your mother.

*On the day of your birth,
your family cried bitterly
at the unfortunate numbers
that meant a white horse woman.
As you fought to climb free
she struggled to hold you in,
knowing even then that you were
too strong to be tamed.
You learned early that men leave,
so you wear years on your back
to prove you have fought,
even when they break your body.*

Halmoni,
at war with the pattern of your life
you refuse to even die quietly.
They call you difficult,
but nod respectfully towards your grave.
On my return home,
the flowers I bring you seem small and few.
As if you remember I fear geckos,
one scampers across your name,
leaving only the memory of instinct.

NATIONALISM AND NATION CONSTRUCTION: FIRST AND THIRD WORLD PROBLEMATICS

In Pai's work, the desire for education motivates Chung Sook's mother Hee Kyung to come to America as a picture bride. Solicited by a go-between, she sees the pictures in her hand less than the mobility they represent. The go-between's "quick reply" of "Yes, I'm certain there is" to her question of the availability of a college marks the initial moment of deception for Hee Kyung, who envisions Hawai'i as a land of promise. Yet the go-between is only one of many conspiring forces that push Hee Kyung towards America; her contact with Methodist missionaries likewise shapes her decision to leave. The missionaries encourage her to better her "political and economic life" and advocate her "spreading the word of God".[13] As Hee Kyung aspires to be American, then, she also satisfies the motives of others who seek to benefit from her actions. Hence the degree of Hee Kyung's agency in her immigration to Hawai'i becomes suspect, rewriting the narrative of immigration as an act of individual will.[14]

Similar to the experience of Haesu in Kim Ronyoung's *Clay Walls,* downward rather than upward mobility characterizes Hee Kyung's movement to and arrival in America. The literal space she occupies in Hawai'i, marking her "below" her servants in Korea, signifies this:

> The moment the bride stepped into her new home, she was overcome with dismay. Only one room to cook and sleep and entertain in. The bare wooden floor. Sparse, crude furnishings. Even the servants' quarters in her home back in Taegu looked

better. She was like a flower rudely transplanted in foreign
soil. . . . Before long she became aware of her husband's meager
wages. She knew she had to abandon her dream of attending
college in Hawaii. (2-3)

As a "flower rudely transplanted," Hee Kyung feels at the mercy of
more powerful forces. Not only does she lose a sense of agency in her
journey from Korea to the U.S., but her initial experience in Hawai'i
undercuts and inverts first world American "privilege" and third world
Korean "disadvantage." What Hee Kyung needs and desires lies in her
upperclass standing *in Korea*; when Chung Sook takes ill, Hee Kyung
seeks medical help in Korea, since, as poor laborers, they cannot access
adequate care in Hawai'i. Furthermore, it is during her return to Korea
that Hee Kyung finally obtains a college education at Ewha University
in Seoul, a school that "[seethes] with nationalism" and where "the
majority of the students were revolutionaries" (17). Along with her
education, then, Hee Kyung gains a renewed sense of her Korean
nationality as Korea becomes a place of empowerment for her. In
contrast, in Hawai'i she cannot attend college because the "urgent task
for her (there) was to learn to cook and sew" (5, my parenthesis).
Instead of finding opportunity in America, Hee Kyung experiences the
erasure of her class privilege as a yangban.

   Although Do In also comes to Hawai'i in hopes for a better life,
his class status shapes the difference between him and his wife. As a
farmer in Korea, he pursues a life in America that will provide the
mobility denied to him in the homeland:

"After I graduated from high school in Andong, I had no means to
go to college. You know, Andong is a small country town. Only
one boy in my school got a scholarship to a college in Tokyo; he
scored the highest in an exam. I was only the second highest. I
was so disappointed. I had nothing to look forward to but farming
with my father." (3)

Despite that Do In sees his move to America as a guarantee of success,
his position upon his arrival in Hawai'i is the same as it is in Korea.
Plantation work offers him the only access to the U.S., so Do In
accepts that he must work in the fields. In fact, his frustration comes
mainly from the duration of time he spends on the plantations, as

opposed to the indignation of poverty and his treatment as a second-class citizen. Tenaciously holding to the American Dream, Do In rejects Koloa plantation in Kauai as a representation of the new world, seeking his fortune on O'ahu instead, intending to begin anew in the "real" America: "We imagined Honolulu was a big, glamorous metropolis. When we first came to Hawaii as *yi-min,* we all dreamed of wealth" (6). Yet once in Honolulu, his situation does not change significantly. Determined to be successful, he works as a yardboy in Mānoa for H. Hackfeld, a rich haole businessman, and sells vegetables in his spare time to earn enough money for a picture bride and a new apartment, both of which he eventually attains.

America nevertheless represents lack, largely because the Kwons occupy an underclass in Hawai'i built along color and class lines. Contained by race and complexion, Hee Kyung and Do In encounter limits despite the fact that the American Dream promises the reinvention of oneself by beginning anew:

> The promise of this new world for them, as F. Scott Fitzgerald portrayed it, was mythic: here an individual could remake himself. . . . [Immigrants] could give themselves new identities by changing their names as did Doris Kapplehoff to Doris Day, Bernie Schwartz to Tony Curtis, Issur Danielovitch to Kirk Douglas, and Edmund Marcizewski to Ed Muskie. . . . Others became "Americans" mainly by shedding their past, their ethnicity—the language, customs, dress, and culture of the old country.[15]

However, as Ronald Takaki points out, the distinguishable foreignness of Asian immigrants, who came from a "different shore," prevented them from entering a "level playing field" the way ethnic whites did. Hee Kyung and Do In both encounter racial prejudice; however, their Korean class standings distinguish their reactions to this racism. The American Dream reads "immigrant" as "lower class," but according to its tenets, one sheds this identity by rising in the new world.[16] Yet if many Korean immigrants came from the middle and upper classes, how does class status in the homeland affect their devolved positions in the new world, especially when there is no desire to shed homeland class identifications?

Hee Kyung's affluent upbringing and Do In's farming background contrast sharply. While Hee Kyung may return to a life of privilege in

Taegu, Do In—at least initially—can only find a farmer's life whether in Korea or Hawai'i.[17] Korean class differences not only shape their experiences in Hawai'i but account for their relationships to Korean nationalism. This, in turn, affects gender roles within their home: Hee Kyung becomes heavily involved in nationalist activities outside, while Do In remains at home to work on his inventions.[18] Disillusioned with life in Hawai'i, Hee Kyung invokes the privilege she possessed in Korea; thus her stake in Korea's independence is greater than her husband's.[19] Meanwhile, Do In continues to protect the notion of the American Dream that allows him the *possibility* of mobility where Korea affords him none. Hence his concern revolves less around the affairs of the homeland than succeeding in the U.S.

As mentioned earlier, Korean nationalism had strong ties to Western Christianity, and in Hawai'i, the two major Korean churches, Korean Methodist Church and Korean Christian Church, were hotbeds of nationalism. While both Hee Kyung and Do In attend church because it "offered all the social, political, and religious life the Kwons needed" (4), it is Hee Kyung who feels religious and nationalist fervor, in part because she maintains an explicit connection to Korea and her privilege through it:

> Despite that she found freedom from Japanese oppression in Hawaii, it was one dreary day after another for Hee Kyung. She tried to find something useful and interesting to do each day. But Sunday was the special day that she looked forward to. . . . Like her new friends, she found immense comfort and solace in the Methodist church. *She believed her religion survived well the transplanting process.* (4, my italics)

Here Christianity functions as a stabilizing force in the movement between nations, and Hee Kyung takes comfort in the "survival" of Christianity in Hawai'i. Her nationalizing of Christianity as Korean, in that it "survived well the transplanting process," appears to diminish the religion's Western origins. Yet the fact that Christianity allowed Koreans to resist the Japanese in the homeland justifies such an identification. Thus if Christianity "transplants" itself to the U.S., it likewise carries resonances of resistance with it. Hee Kyung's comment, then, indicates the transplanting of political position as well: the Korean community, under the protection of Christianity, survives as an oppressed group in the islands in the same way it existed as an oppressed group in Korea. To a large degree, Christianity as it is constructed by Koreans depends on Koreans' subjugated positions. Furthermore, if those most invested in nationalism and Christianity act out of the erasure of their privilege in the U.S., then Christianity also depends on Koreans such as Hee Kyung. In order to continue as an institution, Christianity in Hawai'i must sustain the memory of privilege.

The link for Hee Kyung between religion, nationalism, and privilege becomes explicit when, because of her strong dedication to the cause, the Korean women of her church organization elect her to represent them at the Mansei demonstration, and pool their money to pay for her trip.[20] In other words, Hee Kyung's class privilege, which fuels her nationalist agenda, enables her to return to Korea with Chung Sook to her yangban upbringing. In this border-crossing, Hee Kyung possesses a commodity both valuable and threatening—the privilege gained by simply living in Hawai'i. Power surrounds the notion of America in Korea: when the Japanese arrest and imprison Hee Kyung during the Mansei Rebellion, her father suspects they have detained her because of her affiliation with a "powerful organization" in Hawai'i, although this "powerful organization" consists of "a small group of women, all poor immigrants" (24). By virtue of her association with the U.S., Hee Kyung appropriates its power. Ironically, this power only has significance overseas, outside "official" U.S. borders.

Disruptions of the first and third world binaries suggest Hee Kyung's and Do In's positions in Hawai'i directly relate to their positions in Korea; breakdowns of borders and national constructions necessitate a transnational perspective in analyzing immigrant journeys to America. Basic notions of "immigration"—that immigrants came from poor countries to seek better lives in the U.S.—become problematic if we consider that a system actively seeking cheap Asian labor brings Hee Kyung and Do In to Hawai'i. Wayne Patterson's work, while at times downplaying the role of Japanese colonization in Korean emigration, successfully documents the conspiratorial and illegal machinations of the HSPA in securing Korean contract labor. Because the federal government outlawed contract labor on the continental U.S. in 1885, and in the territory of Hawai'i in 1900, the planters used illicit means to bring Koreans to Hawai'i, since not only was it illegal "to offer a contract to an immigrant before he or she arrived in the United States . . . it was also criminal for an employer to pay transportation to the United States for the immigrant."[21] This law passed due to trade union activity on the continental U.S. that called for the protection of American labor from foreign competition; yet because Hawaii's plantations relied heavily upon foreign labor, this law proved to be a significant obstacle. Thus ironically, the very thing the planters sought—annexation—eventually brought with it contract labor laws hindering sugar production.

The issue of annexation illustrated the military and economic imperialist power of the U.S. As the planters saw it, annexation would expand their profits and markets, since "[p]rohibitive tariffs limited the access of Island sugar to markets garnered during the Civil War period."[22] In 1893, then, they illegally overthrew the Hawaiian nation.[23] When the U.S. officially annexed Hawai'i in 1898, it had done so after much debate. Those in the Senate against it declared racial problems as their chief objection: since Hawai'i had a large nonwhite population, admitting it to the Union would mean "contaminating Anglo-Saxon America with the likes of 'leprous kanakas' and 'mongrel senators.'"[24] Politicians in favor of annexation valued Hawai'i as a strategic military post; the U.S. government, well aware of Japan's desire to control the islands, drafted the annexation treaty in 1897 as "a powerful hands-off warning to Japan, which the McKinley administration believed was about to overthrow or subvert the Hawaiian government."[25] Not only did Hawai'i become the site of conflict for nations; it represented a locus from which the U.S. extended its sphere of influence throughout the Asian and Pacific regions. Given this, we must problematize and explore the notion of the "immigrant success story" in America and specifically Hawai'i by focusing upon the motivating forces behind it. The "immigrant success story" consists of a rags-to-riches paradigm that neglects global factors influencing immigration patterns. If U.S. global politics affected movement to Hawai'i, then to read Korean and other "Local" establishments in the islands as simple success stories risks oversimplification.

Pai's narrative depicts the growing success of Do In as an upholster, an inventor, and ultimately the creator of bamboo drapery. While it might be argued that his success makes him part and parcel of the colonizing capitalist force that has dispossessed Native Hawaiians, this does not sufficiently explain his position in and claim to Hawai'i. With Hawaiian sovereignty[26] calling for a reassessment of Local history and land claims, we must reread Local history—and in this case, Korean history—in order to locate the space in which these claims are held and maintained. Geraldine Kosasa-Terry asserts that Locals must examine "where they are now"—as a privileged population that has built its success on the land of the Hawaiian nation—rather than "how they got there."[27] Calling for a discourse of "settler colonialism," Kosasa-Terry posits that Locals' identification as victims of U.S. colonialism ignores their own positions as colonizers of the kānaka maoli. While I agree that many Locals have elided issues of their complicity in Native Hawaiian dispossession, it is difficult to overlook the fact that *where* Locals are now relates to *how* they got to Hawai'i.

Wilma Sur's work on Korean assimilationist impulses speaks to the issue of Koreans in Hawai'i as oppressors of Native Hawaiians. Demonstrating that Koreans in Hawai'i reacted strongly to the islands' Japanese majority because of the political situation abroad, Sur states that Koreans in opposition to Local Japanese sought alignment with the *haole* structure that ironically oppressed them:

> Significantly, the Koreans found themselves in agreement with the white society in their antipathy towards the Japanese racial stock, providing an important point of agreement between the Korean minority group and the society into which they were aspiring to assimilate. The Koreans could dwell on their anti-Japanese sentiment and make it rather public because it was condoned by the social order under which they lived. It also became an essential political point by which Koreans could distinguish themselves from the Japanese and hopefully prove themselves different: that is, more American.[28]

Hence Koreans resisted alliance with Japanese and by extension Local culture mainly through economic competition and the desire to be like the haole. During the 1920 labor strike that united Japanese and Filipino workers, for instance, Koreans volunteered as strikebreakers. Their decisions came overwhelmingly in reaction to the Japanese massacre of Korean demonstrators in the homeland during the Mansei Rebellion only a year earlier. For these Koreans, Hawai'i existed as a "safe" ground on which they could resist all forms of Japanese influence.

Although Korean emigration to Hawai'i and establishment in the islands were ostensibly the result of Japanese colonialism, it is hard to deny the U.S.'s complicity. In the 1905 Taft-Katsura agreement, the U.S. agreed to turn a blind eye to Japan's designs on Korea in exchange for Japan's "hands-off" policy towards the U.S. occupation of Philippines.[29] Furthermore, despite President Wilson's post-WWI "Fourteen Points," one of which called for the "reestablishment of independent nations in colonized lands," Korean delegates to the Paris Peace Conference were rejected by Wilson, as he had intended the rights to self-determination only for the former colonies of the Austro-Hungarian and German empires.[30] Thus Korean establishment in the islands becomes a by-product of U.S. as well as Japanese colonialism. This does not exonerate Koreans or other non-native peoples in the islands of their participation in the eradication of the Hawaiian nation. I am simply suggesting that to get to the root of non-native resistance to sovereignty, we must undertake a more complex analysis of Local history.

Issues of mobility and economic success pertain here, for it is true that Korean laborers moved off the plantations at a quicker rate than other ethnicities. Bernice Kim notes that although Koreans were the "latest immigrants" to come to Hawai'i aside from Filipinos, "within less than three decades all excepting 458 and their families [had] left the plantations."[31] Perhaps one of the most interesting factors to which Kim attributes this phenomenon concerns the establishment of the Schofield Barracks in Wahiawā. While Chinese and Japanese merchants dominated businesses within the post such as laundries, shoe repairs, and tailors during the first ten years of Schofield's establishment, beginning in 1922, Koreans began to acquire concessions, mainly because army officials favored Koreans over others.

> As a military policy Japanese were discouraged from working on the post so that the entire field was left free for the Koreans. . . . With the beginning of the local depression many Koreans living in Honolulu, and others from plantations have moved into Wahiawa, since it had gained a reputation as a place where Koreans could find jobs.[32]

Because of the military's resistance to Japanese and preference for Koreans, Koreans in Wahiawā succeeded financially off the plantations. In light of Sur's argument, an added bonus to this financial success was that Koreans saw in this arrangement an opportunity to beat the Japanese.

As much as Sur's analysis illuminates the relationship between Koreans' material success in Hawaiʻi and Japanese colonialism in Korea, it is dangerous to draw a simple correlation between success and nationalism in the case of Koreans in Hawaiʻi. While Do In achieves wealth and status for himself and his family, the desire to attain what he could not in Korea motivates him, rather than a nationalist agenda to subvert the Japanese majority in Hawaiʻi. In other words, U.S. and Japanese colonialism strongly dictate his presence in Hawaiʻi, politicizing his wish to succeed in America; yet Do In's motivation does not testify to Korean nationalism per se. Do In seeks social mobility and a home; the home he does achieve comes as a result of strong if not obsessive dedication to work and the American Dream. Ultimately, home and work become inseparable, bringing with them many consequences to the breakdown of their distinctions.

IN SEARCH OF A HOME: CONFLATIONS OF CLASS, GENDER, AND NATIONAL ECONOMIES

The distribution and construction of home and work spaces in Pai's memoir attests to the connection between Do In's residence in Hawaiʻi and his desire to succeed. In the house on Pele street, rented with the earnings from his job as a furniture upholsterer,[33] Do In builds a workshop from a makeshift room under the house where he can work on his inventions. When he returns home from his job in the evenings, he heads "straight for the room under the house to engage in his favorite pastime" (52). His map of Oʻahu, then, consists of his workplace and workshop, with his family space in the background. The division of "work" and "home" is clearly demarcated, and although the workshop is part of the home, the two nevertheless remain separate.

However, the loss of Do In's job anticipates the merging of work and home, as the family must move into a factory in downtown Honolulu where Do In hopes to begin his own business. The segment recounting Do In's unemployment reveals a significant moment of doubt in Pai's memoir, a rupture that interrogates the American Dream's easy equating of hard work with success. While Chung Sook tells us that all is well with Do In's upholstering work, her comment that it goes "[p]erhaps too well" (57) discloses her own anxieties about the business:[34]

> [Do In] was known in the trade as a first-rate upholsterer. Bailey Furniture Company, the most prestigious home furnishing shop in Honolulu and a competitor of Coyne Furniture, lured my father away to their shop by offering him wages and benefits he could not refuse. Then another tempting offer came to him from a man who was opening a new business in town. This man's name was Calistro. . . . The Calistro firm folded about a year after it opened. The year was 1928. (57)

Although the date is significant here, the emphasis is dually upon the effects of the Great Depression and the fact that being a valuable commodity carries its own risks. Bailey and Coyne continue to do good business during this period, and many opportunities arise for Do In. However, his feelings of having "lost face" prevent him from returning. Do In must invent himself once again, but can only do so by opening his own upholstery shop. In the same way he refused Koloa plantation as part of the new world, he discards Bailey and Coyne as his roads to success, as they can only remind him of "failure."

To save money, the family relocates to their new dwelling, a combination factory/ domicile:

> The shop and apartment were located on Beretania Street, opposite the town water pumping station. The store was one in a row of shops in a dilapidated two-story building. To get to our living quarters we had to go through the store; there was no other way because all the shops shared common walls. (76)

Stores rather than homes surround the Kwons, and their living space soon becomes an extension of Do In's work space. Distinctions blur as the children begin to resemble the furniture Do In builds. Consuming and being consumed by their father's work, they soon associate engulfment with prosperity:

> We children lived in the midst of dust. My brothers and I had nowhere to play but in and near the cemented area between the store and the carpenter shop. Inevitably we developed allergies that

remained with us for life. We breathed in the powdery shavings of the
wood saw. We inhaled the exhaust from the hand-grinding machine,
which spewed puffed-up cotton and resilient black hair used for
stuffing furniture. . . . Clouds of dust swirled about continually,
settling in our hair and clogging our noses and lungs. Much of the
dust rose and settled upstairs in our apartment. When my father's
business was very good, we literally bathed in dust. (83-84)

For Do In, securing a home is explicitly tied to the notion of work:
merging the two facilities will eventually provide the family with a
separate home/space. The work area of the factory represents the need to
make a living, yet it also provides an escapist pleasure for Do In: "[Hee
Kyung] left him alone to dwell in his dream world of fancy ideas. He
could come and go as he pleased, slipping into fantasy and returning to
the work in the factory" (89). When Hee Kyung eventually demands a
separation of work and home, she does so in opposition to Do In's
vision of the collapse as necessary: the family's survival depends upon
invention and therefore, this mixture of fantasy and labor. For Hee
Kyung, the combining of home and work takes its toll by trapping her
in endless duties, since not only must she care for the "home," she
must perform all the tasks in the shop "except the carpentering and
painting" (78).

Hee Kyung tries to establish boundaries between home and work
by requesting that Ordway, Do In's employee, pay rent for a room he
keeps above the store. While Do In views Ordway's residence as an
even exchange for the skills his employee has taught him—writing
invoices, addressing customers, and preparing job descriptions—Hee
Kyung's concern revolves around distinguishing between private/home
and public/work.[35] When Do In refuses, Hee Kyung turns to other
means, eventually using Chung Sook as a rationale for their moving
into a house:

> Mother retorted . . . "And it's about time we got out of this prison we
> call home. We can't even hear a visitor knocking on our front door—
> our front door is the front door of the store! We need a parlor so that
> our daughter can receive gentleman callers." (85)

Through such an argument, Hee Kyung appeals to the familial
obligations that Do In has forgotten in the pursuit of success, invoking

the need for domestic space by suggesting its impending degeneration. In other words, if the intended goal of Chung Sook's having gentleman callers is marriage, then Hee Kyung fears the lack of a home will deprive Chung Sook of the opportunity to establish one of her own. Hee Kyung eventually persuades Do In that the family must move; yet when, with the help of a kye, the Kwons do attain a home in Makiki, they feel profoundly uncomfortable with its spaciousness:

> The bedrooms were compact, but the living-dining area was huge. The dining set, a rectangular table with six chairs, looked lost, as if floating in a sea of space. The many windows in the room left little or no wall space for pictures. (92)

The family gains the luxury of privacy, yet this solitude denotes disconnection and isolation, especially given that the Kwons have attained a home when others have not. Because of the Depression, the subdivision remains empty.

Although attaining the home might indicate fulfillment of the American Dream, it is important to remember that the Kwons buy the house with the help of the kye, and not because Do In's upholstery shop has paid off. In fact, in the years after the purchase of the house and preceding Poinciana Draperies, "the mortgage payments and the *kye* dues [weigh] heavily" (93) on the Kwons, indicating that they have *not* reached financial stability. The use of the kye becomes the family's means to achieve when the prescribed routes fail; Hee Kyung's surprise at the effects of the Depression reinforces this point. Believing that poverty and the "struggle to gain a foothold in the economy" plagues only immigrants from the old countries, she is shocked to discover that Americans (whites) are not rich. For her, "America" means "invincibility"; as "outsiders," it makes sense that she and her family must use the kye. While the kye appears to elevate the Kwons' economic position, its power originates from their exclusion from the American Dream, and the presence and power of this exclusion cannot be erased.[36]

However, the home in Makiki brings with it a sense of stability that reestablishes traditional gender roles for Do In and Hee Kyung. Gender transgression diminishes, signaled by the changing forms of Hee Kyung's involvement with Korean nationalism, a movement historically dominated by men. In the record of arrests for the Mansei demonstration, only 1,529 of the 38,909 people arrested were women,[37] yet this was less an indication of political apathy than a reflection of the Confucian ethics that confined women to the home. In *The Dreams of Two Yi-Min,* Hee Kyung's participation in nationalist activities is masculinized at the same time it attempts to resist masculinization and reclaim nationalism by illustrating a woman's involvement. Because wife and husband work together to maintain the home, the gender role slippage caused by Hee Kyung's nationalism fosters and echoes Do In's. Early in Pai's work, when Hee Kyung returns from Korea after the Mansei, it is Do In who reorients her in the domestic space:

> Mother stood in the kitchen a long time without saying a word. She looked lost and a little distressed. Finally, shaking her head, she muttered, "*Ai gu,* I'll have to start cooking again."
>
> Father showed her where he kept the pots and pans, and together they prepared supper. He washed the rice and set the pot on the stove, and Mother selected an assortment of *banchan* from the jars and boxes on the living room floor. . . .
>
> As I was about to fall asleep the first night I overheard my father say, his voice tinged with sadness, "I wonder if our country will ever become a free nation."
>
> Mother replied with passion, "Oh, we can't give up. We must find a way to defeat Japan." (35-36)

Once the Kwons establish themselves in the Makiki household, however, the domestic space contains Hee Kyung's nationalist passions and reinscribes her feminine gender role. Possession of home and wealth eventually assure Do In's role as head of the household, and he reasserts himself sexually and economically by discouraging Hee Kyung's involvement with Kim Soo Han, a handsome singer/showman/patriot from Korea. Although Hee Kyung's relationship with Kim is platonic, it threatens Do In on several levels. The presence of another male in the household primarily endangers his sexual territory; furthermore, Hee Kyung's involvement with Korean nationalism carries associations with Do In's former domestication/feminization. Characterizing Kim as a "parasite," Do In forbids Hee Kyung's friendship with the patriot and demonstrates his own adoption of first world and third world binary constructions. As a part of the first world via financial stability, Do In sees Korea/Korean nationalism/Kim as parasitic, dependent upon the

U.S. for its survival and benefit. Despite his earlier lament over Korea's plight, Do In leaves no room for nationalist dedication here, reading his wife's interest in Kim in purely sexual terms. Hee Kyung ends her friendship with Kim and little mention is made of her political activities or views thereafter, at least until the advent of WWII when she volunteers for the Red Cross like many other Korean women in the islands. Economic stability allows Hee Kyung's participation, as Do In's ability to hire another worker provides her with enough free time to devote to her community activities. Paradoxically, although Do In's financial success circumscribes Hee Kyung's nationalist activities, it also enables them. What validates Hee Kyung's nationalism in this instance, however, is the conflation of pro-Korean and pro-American (hence, anti-Japanese) sentiments. This recontextualizes Korean nationalism for her; as the war effort requires *both* men and women, Hee Kyung enacts no gender transgression in her involvement, and only shows her support for the United States in a time of war. Earlier in the text, Hee Kyung's activism necessitates her domestic absence and displacement, as nationalism and the Mansei removed her from the lives of her parents and her family. Yet during WWII, Hee Kyung's war activities coexist with her domestic duties; while volunteering for the Red Cross, she extensively plans Chung Sook's wedding. Signifying the blend of the two, what little Chung Sook gains of Korean nationalism is in the form of domestic advice, as she understands the importance of marrying "a Korean, not a Japanese" (128).

Financial stability and the Makiki home secure Do In's masculinity in the same way they shape Hee Kyung's femininity. Do In's trade as an upholsterer, and eventually, a maker of draperies, handbags, and hats, appears to feminize[38] him or at least locate his line of work within domestic/feminine spaces: in a chapter entitled "Old Men and Ladies' Handbags," Chung Sook describes her father's wartime business operation of enlisting men to help him make purses out of scrap bamboo pieces. While this might indicate the ways in which war feminizes or disempowers men who do not participate in combat, Do In and his employees *capitalize* on the war and thus support their families. War enables rather than disables these men, and Do In's "feminization" likewise reflects his masculinity in the sense of financial responsibility. This notion also characterizes his success with Poinciana Draperies: though his clients are overwhelmingly rich kamaʻāina women, his financial success allows him to retain his position as head of the household. Do In's success with Poinciana Draperies also gives rise to his disconnection with Korea. Having "made it" in the U.S., Korea's importance as an identifying marker decreases significantly for him. Discovering his ability to achieve the American Dream, he places his loyalties with Hawaiʻi and the U.S. For Do In, the war does not magnify Korean-Japanese tensions; in fact, he has few qualms over conducting business with Japanese merchants. To him, WWII simply means his bamboo shipment from Japan must halt:

> The full impact of war with Japan did not dawn on my father until he learned that all trade between the United States and Japan was cut off. In the immediate reaction of protecting the islands from further attack by Japan, he had not thought of the economic effect of the war. No longer could he import bamboo. No longer could he sell Poinciana Draperies. His big moneymaker was doomed. (124)

Although he participates as a volunteer truck driver in the war years, we hear mostly of his economic profit through the war, not only through bamboo handbags but through other inventions such as blackout curtains. National origins mean less to Do In than wealth and survival, and if the U.S. will provide him with these things, then his allegiance will turn to America. It is this allegiance to the U.S., though, that ironically creates space for his Korean nationalist feelings since once again, anti-Japanese sentiment connects Korea and the U.S. The Kwons "and their compatriots in Hawaii were jubilant beyond words when they learned of Japan's capitulation to the Allies. They rejoiced! They believed Korea would be freed at last of Japan's imperialist rule!" (144); yet from what we see in the text, Do In's concern revolves mainly around financial gain.

If poverty in Hawaiʻi fuels Hee Kyung's earlier nationalist sentiments, it fails to motivate her passion during Kim Soo Han's visit, since Kim arrives during a time in which the Kwons prosper. Hee Kyung confesses that Kim's visit "rekindled the revolutionary fervor and zeal she had felt as a young woman ready to fight against Japanese aggression" (120). Despondent over the fact that in Korea "conditions are worse now," that "[s]o many more Koreans are reduced to poverty," and that the "Japanese are taking from [Koreans] their land, their money and, worst of all, their dignity" (120), Hee Kyung utters words tinged with nostalgia. She discovers during her visit to Korea in the 1930s that "yangban" becomes a signifier robbed of its meaning. Her elaborate preparation and rituals for Chung Sook's wedding become symbols of what has been lost: "[Hee Kyung] sighed, 'In Korea it would be easier. . . . Here, we are the only Kwons'" (152). Yet to be these "Kwons" is to be a part of the U.S., a first world power.

This privilege and power is geographically specific, however. Although racism affects social and economic positions in Hawai'i, the large nonwhite presence in the islands affords a mobility for the Kwons not readily found on the continental U.S. For this reason, the Kwons— and in particular, Chung Sook—find their identities and national affiliations rewritten on the "mainland."[39]

Mainland Haoles

Try listen:
I nevah talk stink about da haoles,
till I went come to da mainland.
Back home, if one haole act up,
dey get bust up, ah?

But I went figure dat in LA,
get plenty Orientals, like dat.
Get plenty, but get plenty
da kine prejudice haoles, too.

Dis one time in Westwood,
one group of haole boys comes up,
and one goes,
"Man, there are too many fucking Orientals in Westwood."

So I gave him stink eye and I went,
"Yeah, and too much white trash, too."
But he nevah went hear me cuz dey was
cracking up.

Dat was my first week in LA.
You know what?

Nevah get better.

Try listen:

On da mainland, plenty whites,
Dey think dey own da place,
but you know what?
They still haoles to me.
You know, da kine foreigners.

"I BELIEVE WE NEED A *HAOLE* FRONT": HAWAI'I AND THE CONTINENT

Asserting that the majority nonwhite population in Hawai'i provides the Kwons with greater mobility does not imply that the islands are a multicultural paradise.[40] Pervading *The Dreams of Two Yi-Min* is a strong sense of Koreanness, community, and racial separatism that makes this idea an impossibility. Koreans in Pai's work recognize and uphold racial divisions, thus dismantling the notion of a harmonious "paradise"; however, the island's racial separatism allows for a greater access to privilege, as seen by the contrast between Do In's business ventures on the continent and in Hawai'i. My intent in this particular section is not to deconstruct the binary between Hawai'i and the continent, but to observe the shifts and negotiations involved in the move between the geographies of Hawai'i and the "mainland."

The marriage between a Korean parishioner's daughter and a man of Japanese ancestry in Hawai'i prompts Chung Sook to marry "a Korean, not a Japanese." The uproar in the Korean community provoked by the union of a Korean and a Japanese causes Chung Sook and her friends to declare that "the prudent thing to do was to avoid dating Japanese boys." For the sake of communal integrity, they likewise rule out Chinese and Caucasian boys; suddenly aware of the extent of what is "unacceptable," they understand their identity as "a small minority among the races in Hawaii" (122). What constitutes the "races in Hawaii" however, is another matter. The failure to mention Filipino, Hawaiian, or Portuguese men indicates that the Korean community has already instituted levels of acceptability; dating these men is unthinkable, hence, unnamed. Chung Sook's and her friends' interpretations of themselves as a "small minority among the races in Hawaii" establishes at the very least a two-tiered hierarchy that puts Korean, Japanese, Chinese, and haole at one level, and Filipino, Hawaiian, and Portuguese at another. The structure of this hierarchy somewhat complicates—though does not negate—the notion that to succeed means to be like the haole. Privilege and whiteness have a complex relationship in Pai's work that an equating of the two cannot characterize. While this assertion appears to rewrite Sur's thesis that Koreans sought to distinguish themselves from Local Japanese by emulating the haole, it in fact elaborates on the difficulties of doing exactly this. Because the Japanese had such a strong influence in Hawai'i, it is difficult to locate privilege and entitlement simply within a haole domain; the Japanese in Hawai'i became a threat *because* they began to rival the haole. Gary Okihiro's *Cane Fires: The Anti-Japanese Movement in Hawaii, 1865-1945* documents the Japanese economic power in Hawai'i, as well as the tactics employed by the state government to keep this power in check. For instance, "Americanization" programs in the 1920s sought to coopt niseis who were replacing isseis in the work force by persuading them to be "good Americans" rather than "good Japanese";[41] and as it may be argued that the Japanese did eventually replace the haole as a ruling power in Hawai'i, simply changing the color of the oppressor, privilege here cannot be linked solely to whiteness.

Some of this is evident in Pai's depiction of language. Speaking "standard" as opposed to "pidgin" English gives Chung Sook entry into an elite system of education, yet she does not see herself as resembling whites. This is especially enlightening given that during this time, Hawaii's government established "English Standard Schools" (ESS). The ESS program translated into a weeding-out process of children who spoke pidgin English—children who were more often than not Local. ESS schools offered more programs and classes, and were better equipped and run. Hence many haole children and standard English-speaking Local children in the islands obtained better educations than their pidgin-speaking counterparts.[42] Significantly, Chung Sook's desire to speak standard English does not come from the haoles around her. Rather, two Korean American girls visiting from Los Angeles serve as her role models for the "lilting speech." Chung Sook's linguistic aspirations immediately pay off; yet despite her pride in her improved eloquence, which earns her the role of "chairman of the school assemblies" at Royal Elementary School (non-ESS), her comment that the "speeches by the (haole) visitors, rendered in standard English, left *us* unmoved, and only the teachers laughed at the jokes" (48, my parenthesis and italics) indicates her resistance to an alliance with the haole speakers of standard English. Her separation from them culminates in the fact that although Chung Sook attends Lincoln Junior High (ESS) because of her improved language skills, she still does not associate standard English with whiteness.

Even Do In, who realizes that his poor English skills hinder his ability to conduct business, sees language acquisition as a tool, rather than a means to be on a par with his wealthy haole clients. Content to have Ordway speak with customers, Do In does not feel the need to improve his English. When Ordway leaves, however, Do In unsuccessfully attempts to imitate "the cadences in [his clients'] speech" (108). At the same time, satisfied with his customers' trust and respect at this level of English, he sees little need to learn more than the bare minimum required. Whereas a novel such as Chang-rae Lee's *Native Speaker* as well as a number of other Asian American works reflect anxiety and shame over accents and speech patterns that reveal foreignness, Pai's work invokes none of this. The Kwons aspire toward material wealth and financial stability, yet do not see these as providing entry into a specific racial stratum. Nor does Pai depict the Kwons as those who endorse or even desire to cast off ethnic signifiers. For what Do In seeks to accomplish, this discarding is unnecessary. He becomes a major contender in the local furnishing industry, and as a result, seeks to expand his business to new territory—the mainland.

But Do In's formula for success in Hawai'i does not translate neatly to San Francisco, as the Kwons' identities are altered and recontextualized. The issue of "proper" English arises again to indicate this: Chung Sook wonders if Do In would "be able to communicate in his pidgin English with people in a sophisticated city" (171), and through her concern, alerts us to her awareness of the difference between kama'āina haoles and continental whites, as well as the relationships she and the family may have to both. For Chung Sook, standard English functions as a shield. Her concern for Do In harkens to two of her own experiences—first, the early days at Royal School when she had not yet learned to speak English; and second, her desire to speak like the two Korean American girls from Los Angeles. Both instances reflect Chung Sook's feelings of inferiority and reveal her fear that Do In will likewise experience feelings of subordination. However, she leaves space for the possibility of her escape from "Otherness" on the continent because her language skills are superior to her father's. In this sense, English becomes a new signifier, providing acceptance by and entry into the world of mainland haoles.

As in Hawai'i, home and work spaces reflect the positions of the Kwons here. Chung Sook and her husband find their apartment on Pacific Avenue to be cold, smelly, and unwelcoming, but because their agenda is business, Chung Sook's experience in the apartment takes less priority: they are not in San Francisco to build a home. The next morning, however, when Chung Sook discovers the location of the shop, she conveys her sense of shock and dismay:

> I suddenly felt overcome with disenchantment. I struggled to get out of the car. How could Father have done a thing like this? Where were his senses when he leased this place? Would any fashionably dressed San Franciscans think of coming down here to buy something beautiful for their homes? I could see derelicts nearby at the corner of Sixth and Mission streets, sharing a bottle of wine. (174)

The Kwon business exists literally outside the borders of the "sophisticated" city. The horror felt by Chung Sook comes from her resistance to the idea that, rather than a "small minority among the races," she has become part of the marginal and rejected, witnessed by the "derelicts" who share "a bottle of wine" down the street from their store and a man presumed to be dead lying outside the front door. The location of the factory on the fringes of what she perceives to be San Francisco predicts the fact that most of the Kwons' clients will come from outside the metropole, from as far away as Bakersfield, thus redefining "success" on the "mainland." Significantly, their first customer is a "former Honoluluan" who remembers Poinciana Draperies from his time in Hawai'i and thus reestablishes and relies upon the family's island identity. Yet business remains slow, as Chung Sook notices that "would-be customers who braved their way" into the shop would leave upon seeing "an Oriental in [the] showroom" (178). For the business to flourish, then, Chung Sook and her husband must remain in the background, in the shadow of a "*haole* front."

Although Ordway serves to some degree as a "haole front" in Hawai'i, the text indicates that his value to Do In comes primarily from his business smarts and his command of standard English rather than his appearance. In contrast, the "blond Miss Shelley" acts as a lure for potential customers by counterbalancing Korean "foreignness" with an "all-American" iconic charm:

> So we hired an attractive young girl with golden hair framing her face, a peaches-and-cream complexion, and a pretty smile. It was amazing how quickly the drop-in trade improved. The blond Miss Shelley greeted customers with a most disarming smile. She spoke to them with ease, and oohed and aahed with them over the beauty of Poinciana. . . . By Thanksgiving Day—four months after our arrival—our factory was humming. We had gained a small foothold in the San Francisco economy. (178)

Chung Sook's decision to hire Miss Shelley takes place after her own experiences of racism in San Francisco that invalidate the protection provided by her ability to speak standard English. Most of these instances occur within department stores, places in which it is conceivable that purchasing power might safeguard Chung Sook. Despite her identity as the daughter of a successful businessman in Hawai'i, however, Chung Sook finds that her mistreatment in these stores results from her racial identity, as the visual becomes extremely powerful by marking her ethnically: she notes that with her "Oriental face" in a "sea of *white* faces," she finds it difficult to flag down salesgirls (175). The choice to italicize "white" here denotes her new color-consciousness, the beginning of her awareness that yellow means "less" on the mainland. Although she does find respite in I. Magnin, she does so in the company of "Indian women in graceful saris leisurely strolling about, and richly gowned Chinese matrons, bejeweled with jade," as well as a few "pigtailed Japanese girls" (176). That the exotic nature of the customers comforts her further indicates her sense of difference here. In addition, her comfort comes both figuratively and literally at a cost, since the merchandise at I. Magnin is "higher priced," indicating that wealth is a key factor in the presence of these women in San Francisco's department stores. There is literally no space for poor women of color here.

The blow to Chung Sook's economic identity manifests itself in her reconstruction of Poinciana's success in Hawai'i as "amateur." When a representative from the *San Francisco Chronicle* looks over the

Poinciana ad, Chung Sook assumes that his boredom and stand-offishness come from her inexperience rather than her race. The ad, which "had worked well . . . in Honolulu" (176), becomes a symbol of her own misplaced, "unsophisticated" position in San Francisco, something whose remedy is the appropriation of whiteness through the hiring of a "haole front." The italicizing of "haole" in Chung Sook's announcement to her husband that they should hire Miss Shelley serves as the textual counterpoint to the italicizing of "white" earlier in the chapter. By calling attention to Chung Sook's use of "haole" here, Pai defamiliarizes the word and forces the reader to reassess its use and definition. Chung Sook's deployment of the term here invokes the privilege in Hawai'i that she cannot access as an "Oriental" in San Francisco; by hiring the *"haole"* Miss Shelley, Chung Sook reestablishes a relationship in which Miss Shelley becomes the "foreigner." In order to do this, however, Chung Sook must in exchange identify as "Local."

Because "Local" has been at odds with "Korean" in Hawai'i, Chung Sook must accomplish several things in order to identify as a Local on the continent: she must erase constructions of Korean racial separatism in Hawai'i; invoke cultural specificity on the continent, hence resisting a totalized Asian ethnicity; and enforce "mainland"/'Local" differences. In doing this, she experiences the rewriting of her identity once again. This affects her relationship to Otherness: as she prepares to leave San Francisco, she identifies a man she sees in the street as a "man from China" rather than a "Chinese man," thus conflating his ethnicity with his nationality. This precludes her connection to him—he becomes an "immigrant" while she retains her "Americanness," despite the fact that she spent her childhood years in Korea and came to Hawai'i speaking a "babble of rapid Korean" (45). Taking further account of their differences, she notes that while she is bundled up in warm clothing, the Chinese man wears nothing but a pair of pants and a gloves as he carries in a shipment of beef. When she asks him whether he is cold, he responds with, "'This nicee . . . I likee!'" (180). His response serves two purposes. It turns San Francisco's (racial) climate into a manifestation of physical discomfort, so that Chung Sook must guard herself against it while the Chinese man has become accustomed to it. Chung Sook's frequent comments on the cold in San Francisco contrast with her longing for the warmth of Hawai'i, and soon signify much more than actual weather. Secondly, it draws attention to language differences between continental "broken" English and Hawaii's pidgin English, and necessarily evokes differing histories behind the languages. In the final contact we see Chung Sook have with another Asian from the continent, she distinguishes herself from him and declares him and his political and social identity as something apart from her own. In this way she prepares herself for a return to the islands, where her identity will change once again.

An ostensibly Local sensibility does not mark Chung Sook's return to Hawai'i, although she expresses a good deal of dissatisfaction with the Korean community, mainly through her father's engagement to Mrs. Chun after Hee Kyung dies in a car accident. While we sense her ambivalence to Koreans and the community previously through her comments about "these people" and the fact that she was never "proud to be a Korean because the feeling had not been instilled in [her]" (121), she desires an explicit disconnection from them only after her return from the continent. As pressure from the community had determined her own marriage choices, it determines her father's: she feels disgust that the "Methodists" (Koreans) interfere with her father's marriage to Mrs. Chun on the basis of the impropriety involved in Mrs. Chun's nursing him back to health after his debilitating accident. Compounding Chung Sook's growing impulse to escape Koreans and the community is Do In's strong sense of filial piety that traps her into running his business. As these two events involve "propriety" and "Koreanness," Chung Sook's reaction to them attests to the continuance of her conflicted feelings over her identity as a Korean in Hawai'i.

"LOSING THE GAMBLE": THE NECESSITY OF FAILURE

Pai concludes her memoir with a series of rapid-fire disasters that in essence tear the family and business apart. As Do In's body begins to fail, so does the business. The quick downfall of Poinciana both narratively and in "real time" destroys the "immigrant success story" cultivated earlier throughout the work by revealing its underside: because success in a capitalistic society comes at the expense of others, the American Dream both requires and demands failure. Perhaps the most glaring proof of this comes from *LS*, a "recent arrival from California," who infringes upon Do In's patent of Poinciana and makes a fortune in Honolulu selling cheaper, lesser-quality versions of bamboo drapery. *LS*'s destruction of Do In's business signals the continuing economics of a system designed to outsell the competition through global exploitation: *LS*'s goods are manufactured in the Philippines and Hong Kong. The legacy of the plantation system is more than a mere ghost here. Not so coincidentally, in the 1950s corporations such as Libby and Del Monte had already staked out "cheap-land areas in the Caribbean and Asia," threatening Dole's pineapple monopoly[43] and preserving a formula for success based on the exploitation of cheap foreign labor.

The irony of Do In's business failing in San Francisco, and *LS*'s success on the West Coast and in Hawai'i attests to lack of protection provided even for those who remain loyal to the American Dream. Although Do In takes legal action against *LS*, the time required to "scrutinize the patent" allows *LS* to flood the market with his own products, rendering the patent system useless for Do In. The effects of this business disaster and others physically disable Do In, whose health fails rapidly and who dies suddenly. Chung Sook and her sister find themselves inheritors of a business their brothers refuse, yet before weighing their options, the business burns to the ground. This event leads to Pai's epilogue, a brief passage reflecting several irreconcilable ideologies in the battle to create a seamless narrative of success.

Chung Sook begins by informing the reader of her and her siblings' career endeavors. Her brothers Young Mahn and Young Chul become a "successful" certified public accountant and a minister "much loved by his parishioners" (196), respectively. Her sister Chung Hee earns her law degree and opens a law office, and Chung Sook teaches high school English, pursuing the career that most interested her. This section of the epilogue seeks to establish a sense of survival/arrival for the Kwon children despite earlier tragedies and struggles. In order to enforce this idea, however, the detrimental forces of war, capitalism, and generational differences must recede in the narrative, yet their overwhelming influence will not easily subside. Pai's use of the words "but" and "however" suggest this. Hee Kyung and Do In "attained their dreams for the good life" through "hard work, great sacrifice, and ultimate joy"; *however,* Korea remained a country whose freedom was "only partially realized." Chung Sook's parents' "inherent honesty, integrity, and goodness served them well," *but* the Old World and filial piety "drove [Do In] into conflict in achieving the good life for his children" (196). In the first statement, Chung Sook suggests survivors' guilt and implies that the connections between Korea and the U.S. are so strong that Korea's political traumas haunt the "good life in [Hee Kyung's and Do In's] adopted land." Her parents do not so much recreate themselves and begin anew, therefore, as they carry the weight of Korean nationalism on their backs in their search for success. In the second statement, Chung Sook criticizes the "Old World" values of filial piety that restrain her and her siblings, yet softens this by ending her epilogue the way she begins it: by showing that Do In nevertheless "did not fail [his children]." An unresolved mixture of the American Dream, Korean nationalism, and filial piety surfaces, yet this is the very point of Pai's work. There are no neat endings here, only the constant negotiation of boundaries and identity. Pai does not uphold or celebrate the ideology of individualism here, but illustrates its ruptures; in this way, she subverts the happy ending of an "immigrant success story."

NOTES

1. In April of 1905, however, the Korean government halted Korean emigration. Many factors, including reports of mistreatment on the plantations as well as Japanese power in Korea, contributed to this decision. In 1912, emigration resumed. Beginning 1906, the plantation owners began to look into Filipino labor as a replacement for Koreans. See Wayne Patterson, *The Korean Frontier in America: Immigration to Hawaii 1896-1910* (Honolulu: University of Hawai'i Press, 1988).

2. See Takaki, *Pau Hana* for more on racial systems within plantation labor society.

3. Ibid. Founded in 1894, the HSPA grew out of the Planters' Labor and Supply Company (est. 1882), whose aim was to fix wages for plantation laborers, provide labor, and protect the contract labor system. The HSPA took on as additional objectives the centralization of management information and decision-making, and agricultural research. After the termination of the contract labor system in the 1900's, the HSPA took new measures to ensure that contract labor would continue in the islands.

4. Patterson, 35.

5. Ibid.

6. Because of Japan's interest in Hawai'i, the Japanese government strongly discouraged Korean immigration, knowing that a large Korean population could rob the Japanese workers of their majority power.

7. For more on the HSPA's conspiratorial and illegal actions concerning recruitment of Koreans, see Patterson.

8. Takaki, *Strangers*, 56.

9. The Asian bachelor societies in the U.S. have been attributed to a number of factors, including the sojourner mentality, in which men traveled the U.S. expecting to make their fortunes then return to Asia, and, in the case of the Chinese, the Page Law that prohibited the entry of Chinese women. See Takaki, *Strangers*.

10. The role of missionaries in the emigration of Koreans is varied and problematic. While some encouraged Koreans to escape the oppressive Japanese rule, others did not wish to see their congregations depart. Furthermore, a few missionaries became involved in the illegal contracting of Korean labor for Hawaii's plantations, in hopes of spreading their religious influence to the islands. See Patterson for more on missionaries in Korea.

11. Alice Chai, "A Picture Bride from Korea: The Life History of a Korean American Woman in Hawaii," *Bridge: An Asian American Perspective* (1979): 2.

12. Takaki, *Strangers*, 72.

13. Margaret K. Pai, *The Dreams of Two Yi-Min* (Honolulu: University of Hawai'i Press, 1989), 4. All subsequent text quoted from Pai shall have page numbers listed parenthetically.

14. It is interesting that, during the present time of strong anti-immigrant sentiment and backlash, immigrant narratives are constructed accordingly to justify racism, exclusion, and xenophobia. Sumida notes that initially, the stereotype of Asian immigrants as sojourners looking to get rich in America was used to condemn Asian Americans as unassimilable members of society. However, this eventually transformed into a perception of Asians as willing immigrants and permanent settlers to the U.S., thereby indicating their propensity towards "selling out" and giving credence to the "model minority myth." See Sumida, "Postcolonialism," 283-284.

15. Takaki, *Strangers*, 12.

16. Ibid., 419. This notion changed dramatically with the lifting of immigration restrictions in 1965. During this time period, many Asian immigrants were highly trained and skilled professionals from middle and upper classes, seeking employment in technological fields in the U.S.

17. Such class differences in marriage were not unusual in light of the fact that many of the Koreans who did emigrate were, unlike the Chinese and Japanese immigrants before them, from varied social classes. Because the

HSPA desired field workers, many Koreans wishing to immigrant listed their occupations as farmers, although only one-seventh of the immigrants actually worked farms in Korea. Dr. Samuel S. O. Lee, ed., *Their Footsteps: A Pictorial History of Koreans in Hawaii Since 1903* (Honolulu: The Committee on the 90th Anniversary Celebration of Korean Immigration to Hawaii, 1993), 30.

18. While women did participate in nationalist activities in Korea and abroad, men constituted the majority of patriots. Hence Hee Kyung's father chastises her for her involvement in "political matters," implying that she has overstepped the confines of femininity. Her sister, on the other hand, is a "quiet lady at home." See Pai, 25.

19. The parallel between Haesu and Hee Kyung persists, given that Haesu's indignation at being treated as a second-class citizen in the U.S. despite her yangban status in Korea drives her passion for nationalism. Chun, like Do In, comes from the lower classes in Korea, and remains dispassionate about Korean nationalist activities. See Kim Ronyoung, *Clay Walls* (Seattle: University of Washington Press, 1987).

20. The Mansei Rebellion took place in Korea on March 1, 1919. A peaceful mass demonstration against Japanese rule, the demonstration lasted three days. Japanese soldiers responded brutally to the demonstrators, torturing, maiming, and murdering them despite the fact that the protesters were unarmed.

21. Patterson, 23.

22. Noel J. Kent, *Hawaii: Islands Under the Influence* (Honolulu: University of Hawai'i Press, 1983), 43.

23. For more on the history of genocide and colonization culminating in the overthrow of the Hawaiian Nation, see *Act of War: The Overthrow of the Hawaiian Nation,* dir. by Puhipau and Joan Lander, 58 min., Na Maka O Ka 'Āina in association with the Center for Hawaiian Studies, University of Hawai'i at Mānoa, 1993.

24. Kent, 65.

25. William Michael Morgan, "The Anti-Japanese Origins of the Hawaiian Annexation Treaty of 1897," *Diplomatic History* 6.1 (1982): 25.

26. Hawaiian sovereignty is a complex issue consisting of many different positions on its formulation. See Roger MacPherson Furrer, ed., *He Alo Ā He Alo: Hawaiian Voices on Sovereignty* (Honolulu: The Hawai'i Area Office of the American Friends Service Committee, 1993).

27. Geraldine E. Kosasa-Terry, "Diasporic Spaces: Rethinking Sites of Immigration/Countering the Narrative of a Nation" (paper presented at the

"Configuring Pacific Diasporas: Indigenous and Immigrant Communities" conference sponsored by the Association of Asian American Studies, Honolulu, 26 March 1996).

28. Wilma Sur, "Korean Ethnic Nationalism," *Hawaii Pono Journal* Fourth Quarter (1970): 22.

29. For more on the Taft-Katsura Agreement, see Patterson.

30. Sucheng Chan, xxix.

31. Bernice Kim, "The Koreans In Hawaii," (master's thesis, University of Hawai'i, 1937), 169.

32. Ibid., 175.

33. Ibid., 162-163. Many Koreans who worked at Coyne Furniture had had no previous experience with or special training for upholstering. Their jobs there came as a result of a Korean friend's connections there.

34. This phenomenon rings of the model minority myth. When Asian Americans began achieving success in schools, they were rewarded with the title of "model minority." At the same time this title appeared to signify arrival, it neglected to mention the glass ceilings Asians would encounter in employment and politics. In addition, the term "model minority" was used to counter the gains of the Civil Rights movements, with the intent to validate the American Dream for those who argued that prejudice on the basis of race, gender, class, and sexuality prevented them from attaining the American Dream. See Curtis Chang, "Streets of Gold: The Myth of the Model Minority," in *Rereading America*, ed. Gary Columbo, Robert Cullen, and Bonnie Lisle (Boston: Bedford, 1992), 54-64.

35. Hee Kyung's purchasing of property for home rentals later in the memoir can therefore be seen as further establishing as well as moving beyond a concept of domestic space.

36. The 1992 Los Angeles Riots brought to light the resentment many felt towards Korean Americans in Koreatown. While public perception hailed and resented Korean Americans for being the "model minority" with purchasing power greater than their African American and Latino counterparts, this perception elided issues of Korean communal collaboration through *kyes* and through unpaid family employment. This resulted in the misconception that Korean Americans were greedy, independently wealthy storeowners who refused to hire Latinos and African Americans out of racism. See Sumi K. Cho, "Korean American vs. African American: Conflict and Construction," in *Reading Rodney King/Reading Urban Uprising*, ed. Robert Gooding-Williams (New York: Routledge, 1993), 196-211.

37. Shannon McCune, *The Mansei Movement* (Honolulu: The Center for Korean Studies, University of Hawai'i, 1976), 33.

38. Many feminist critics rightfully object to the use of this word, particularly because it assigns value to masculinity and constructs femininity as "less." However, I use the word here in order to delineate the ways in which Do In's work slips in and out of traditional gender constructions.

39. I use this term in quotes here to question the prioritizing of the continental U.S. over Hawai'i. In the discourse of Hawaiian sovereignty, the term of choice is "continent." However, I will continue to use "mainland" when Pai uses such terminology, and "continent" when bespeaking concepts of my own.

40. Perhaps the strongest evidence of this is the plantation labor system, in which different ethnic groups continually benefited and also lost at the expense of other groups. While a case could be made for Locals joining together in solidarity and harmony, this reading of Local history in Hawai'i is grossly simplistic and ignores the hierarchy within the structure of Local society.

41. For more on the Americanization programs aimed at Local nisei, see Gary Okihiro, *Cane Fires: The Anti-Japanese Movement in Hawaii, 1865-1945* (Philadelphia: Temple University Press, 1991), 129-162.

42. See Okihiro, *Cane Fires,* 138-141.

43. Kent, 107.

CHAPTER 3

Liberation, Exile, and Border-Crossing
Ty Pak's *Guilt Payment*

2.5

Waiting for her becomes an exercise in difference. Amidst bodies like and unlike my own, I help them take stock of the unfamiliar features, mannerisms, and articles of clothing that add up to the one thing we share— the belief that I don't belong. On the corner of 8th and Olympic in an air conditioned mall, two tall women disguise their curiosity as boredom, sniffing sharply to indicate my dismissal. Others just stare—still others don't care. Just a visitor to Koreatown, like they often get.

She's late. Cultural guide, cultural shield, legitimator, proof of my blood. Proof I'm not Japanese, proof I'm not hapa, proof that like them, I turn when I hear the word yobo. She has asked to meet me here to buy me groceries—what Korean mothers do to show their love. Each month I drive from the Westside, losing my blood on the 10. Once on the Promenade I cussed a drunk Irish who called me a chink, spat the words in his face I'm Korean. No it's not the same. Just like Irish and English.

Tagging along behind her in aisles of hangul, I defer to her in ways she used to long for. I amuse her now, though she doesn't miss a beat—They're first generation, you're almost third—and drops a bag of pears in the cart. She buys everything but kimchee—her own in the trunk—and my car smells for

59

two days, like it usually does. After saying our goodbyes, I'm back on the
10, heading to the Westside, Santa Monica, West LA, Korean on the way.

My mother used to call herself a "gypsy"—someone who wandered, someone who had no home, no roots. What she meant, she told me, was that she was between countries, between languages. Her thoughts came to her sometimes in English, sometimes in Korean, but neither language fit anymore. When she said these things, I envisioned her as the ocean, the stretch of endless water between Korea and Hawai'i.

Unlike my island-born father, she immigrated to the U.S. in 1959. She told me story upon story of her culture shock, how everyone treated her like a poor, third-world refugee. It didn't occur to me until years later how much she'd taken it upon herself to make things easier for my sister and me. If she acculturated, then we didn't have to. Fluent in English, she raised us as English-speakers. I think now of how she must have always been translating. My father knew very little Korean, and between the two of them, the words they passed on to us were words of food, words of care, and words of discipline. But the rest, the rest was English.

But I was Korean, because I wasn't Japanese or Chinese like the other Oriental kids I knew.[1] I was Korean—but not with my mother's side of the family. They were *Korean* Korean. At family parties, the group usually split into two: the Korean speakers, the English speakers. I stayed with my father's relatives who spoke English, sometimes pidgin. They felt different to me, even looked different. Comfortable, familiar. There we were at Christmases and New Years: the Kwons, the Kims, the Changs, all of us Korean. But there was a difference. There still is.

Koreans in Hawai'i fall into two main groups. There are the descendants of plantation laborers and pictures brides from the early part of the century, and the post-1965 immigrants, who significantly outnumber the first group.[2] The higher visibility of the post-1965 immigrants contributes to the perception of Koreans as new arrivals to the U.S., consequently giving rise to the marginalization of Koreans—including the older, more established generations—within Local culture. Many of them survivors of the Korean War, the newer immigrants came to Hawai'i not to escape Japanese persecution, but a country divided by politics and corruption.[3] As much as Japanese colonization informed the experiences of island Koreans during the first wave of immigration to Hawai'i, the Korean war played a role both in the presence of Korean immigrants during the 1960s and in their relationships to Local society. Ty Pak depicts this influence in his collection of short stories, *Guilt Payment.*[4] In his work, he speaks to acts of survival. Often violent and disturbing, his stories convey the difficulty in resolving two very divergent experiences: resisting death and torture in Korea, and living in Hawaii's more often than not peaceful communities. My main objective in this chapter will be to pinpoint and investigate various constructions of and tensions between "American," "Local," and "Korean" identities through two broadly related arguments: that a number of the stories in *Guilt Payment* attempt to make "payment" or reparations to those who did not survive in Korea, and that this "payment" influences conceptions of "Korean American" and "Local"; and that because war makes identification largely situational, stable national identities are overthrown and questioned through a variety of means even in "peaceful" and "nonthreatening" environments. Furthermore, because Pak's stories display the brutality of war on the bodies of women, I will examine women as vehicles of border-crossing in his works. This inquiry into the historical factors that brought Koreans to the islands, as undertaken by Pak, will further illuminate the perception of Koreans in Hawai'i as both participants of and outsiders to Local culture.

Idiom
      —for Nancy

And then she is laughing
having missaid an idiom:
Get on your ball
though this makes sense to me.
I imagine the taming
involved in discipline,
something that feels like
a bear on a ball,
balanced and delicate
for fear of a whip—
sometimes I hear how
she speaks like my mother,
whose language is framed

by too many borders
and then not enough. Between
dawn's early light and
the morning calm, she
dreams of her tongue, yet
for now she will tell me
her childhood is locked
in words of hangul
she has now forgotten, though
they haunt her sometimes
when she is silent; and
hearing her voice
I watch how she stands
balancing on a treacherous surface
threatening the fall,
the crack of the whip
demanding that she indeed perform—
that she tame the wild tongue
that twists in her mouth:
to command and to master
for fear of revolt.

HAHN, THE KOREAN WAR, AND THE POST-1965 IMMIGRANTS

The strong presence of the Korean War in Ty Pak's stories necessitates a brief overview of that historical event. Unable to escape memories and repercussions of the war, Pak's characters seek lives away from the homeland yet carry with them their feelings of *hahn*. A Korean word that has virtually no English equivalent, hahn resembles a deep weariness, grief, or depression that comes from years of oppression and hardship, and expresses a heartfelt sorrow yet endurance that functions in a racially collective manner. During the 1992 Los Angeles Riots, for instance, Korean Americans who felt themselves victimized by a system that saw them as expendable understood their "psychic damage" as hahn.[5]

Historically, Korea has suffered under tremendous control by other countries. When Japan surrendered to the Allied nations on August 15, 1945, Koreans felt they would finally regain independence of the homeland.[6] Yet shortly after this event, the Soviet Union advanced into northern Korea, occupying its major cities. The U.S., fearing a "communist takeover," sent forces to Inchon and subsequently stationed troops over the southern portion of the peninsula. Many Koreans hoped the country's division into two along the 38th parallel would be a temporary measure. However, after Soviet forces blocked areas of northern Korea, refusing to allow the U.N. to carry out its mission to aid Korea in the creation of an independent government, they established the Provisional People's Committee for North Korea in opposition to the U.N.-sponsored government in the south. Because much of the heavy industries were formed in the north during the Japanese occupation, military power was rather easy to develop, and when North Korea crossed the 38th parallel in 1950, they found easy targets in the unprepared south.

Bruce Cumings argues that this attack did not so much launch the Korean War, as commonly narrated by many historians; rather, complex civil disputes between the north and the south culminated in military conflict. Consequently, in the events preceding North Korea's invasion, the U.S. and Russia rallied around pre-existing political differences in Korea.[7] While Cumings provides an insightful and thought-provoking thesis here, the risk lies in downplaying the inherent tensions in a postcolonial "moment" for Koreans liberated from the Japanese after World War II, as well as the forcefulness of U.S./Russian armed occupation. Civil opposition in Korea certainly existed, yet did so as a direct reaction to foreign colonization, of which the U.S. and Russia fully took advantage. What remains clear, nevertheless, is that Korea's troubles were far from over. Independence became, once again, a distant dream.

The war would last three years, devastating the country. One report cites that

> South Korean casualties in the fighting alone are estimated at 150,000 dead, 200,000 missing, and 250,000 injured, while more than 100,000 civilians were abducted to North Korea and the number of war refugees reached several million. North Korean casualties were several times these figures. . . . [D]amage to property has been estimated at something over 3 billion (1953 U.S.) dollars. About 43% of manufacturing facilities, 41% of electrical generating capacity, and 50% of the coal mines in South Korea were destroyed or damaged.

One-third of the nation's housing was destroyed, and substantial proportions of the country's public buildings, roads, bridges, ports, and the like also were reduced to ruins.[8]

To make matters worse, during the war and after, Syngman Rhee instituted an increasingly authoritarian government and began to "strong-arm" his opponents. Because many assembly members feared opposing him, they approved many of his provisions, including one that would exempt him from the prohibition against more than two terms as president. High inflation after the war doubled the price of commodities every six months, and when Rhee and the South Korean government began to favor a select group of industrialists, granting loans and other benefits to them, small businesses went bankrupt. The economic gap between the new business tycoons and rural sectors grew wider and wider, and many Koreans found themselves struggling for their livelihoods. Rhee was eventually driven out of office in 1960 after a number of bloody demonstrations led by university students and professors, yet left a great deal of damage in his wake. When the U.S. finally lifted the ban against Asian immigrants in 1965 that had been in place since 1924, many Koreans were ready to leave for the U.S.

Less identifiable as political exiles than their predecessors, many of the post-1965 group of Korean immigrants came to the U.S. for several reasons: 1) economic betterment, 2) self-development, 3) educational opportunity for their children, 4) political instability in their country, 5) "social absurdity" of their society, and 6) reunion with family and relatives.[9] Many of them highly educated professionals, they differed from earlier plantation immigrants in that they did not seek to escape a colonial regime. However, the significant role of the war in their decisions to leave Korea should not be underestimated: "The fear of war, as an example of 'political instability,' is so serious for Korean emigrants that they are willing to pay any price, no matter how high, to escape from the place of danger, Korea."[10] For those able to leave Korea and reside in the U.S., a "Korean American" identity became a privileged classification indicating two things: 1) they had survived the war; and 2) they had been privileged enough to make the journey to the U.S.

Yet complicating this privileged position was the hardship that many Korean immigrants faced once in the U.S. Because of language difficulties and cultural disorientation, [11] many Koreans experienced a "drastic occupational devolution," taking jobs that had little bearing on their professional training and experience.[12] That several occupations required graduation from an accredited American school as a condition for licensing examinations further closed doors for Koreans.[13] In addition, their decrease in earnings was additionally burdened by their tendency to reside in urban areas, where housing is expensive in a state already known for its high cost of living. Assimilationist social programs of the 1970s failed to adequately accommodate the needs of Asian immigrants, contributing to feelings of social isolation, culture shock, and exclusion.[14] Hence island Koreans relied heavily upon Korean community activities, especially church functions, as well as a network of friends and family to act as stabilizing forces.

These conditions explain the formation of a separate Korean community in Hawai'i, although extremely high outmarriage statistics at the time would seem to indicate a larger degree of integration instead. According to one study, island Koreans had one of the highest rates of interethnic marriage between 1960 and 1974,[15] yet this survey does not distinguish between island-born Koreans and immigrant Koreans. Given this, it might be accurate to say that while the older, more established generations of Koreans have outmarried, newer generations of Koreans set themselves apart from Local society. Certainly figures indicating that second and third generation Koreans in Hawai'i marry partners outside their own ethnic group would support this notion.[16] Specifying which Koreans outmarry helps to explain the perception of Koreans as non-Locals: their ethnic identities are either foreign, distinct, and "FOB," as in the case of the post-1965 group; or "Local" and subsumed by the multiethnic milieu.

The greater visibility of Koreans due to the post-1965 immigrants forces Local communities to contend with their presence, as isolated as that presence may be. Numbers in this case make up for ethnic separation—as of 1976, Korean immigrants were the second largest group entering Hawai'i, and their rate of increase was higher than any other Asian immigrant group.[17]

> For the first time in decades it is commonplace to hear Korean spoken in public places. In schools, hospitals, and social agencies it is the new immigrants who are the focus of special attention and are thought of as the Koreans in Hawaii by others. With more than thirty Koreans (most of them new immigrants) on

the faculty of the University of Hawaii at Manoa alone, the new
immigrants have an articulate leadership which can ably demand
and gain respect for the ethnic integrity of the Koreans when
necessary from those in established sources of power, such as the
media.[18]

While Harvey and Chung contend that the "surviving early immigrants"
and their descendants see the newer immigrants nostalgically as
reminders of their past, culture, and history, I would argue that
differences between the two groups also give rise to a tension based on
claims to Local identity. Koreans fall by the wayside in most accounts
of Local plantation history, and the impact of the newer Korean
immigrants unfortunately threatens to weaken an already tenuous hold.
Thus while established Koreans may in fact feel a revival of their
cultural connections, they also resist conflation of their identities with
those of the post-1965 group. This is not to place blame on the newer
immigrants or argue that they jeopardize Local Koreans' cultural
claims. Rather, my aim is to account for the marginalization of
Koreans within Local culture and to reflect upon the social dynamics
that make this exclusion possible.

In the same way that Local Koreans may distinguish themselves
from the newer immigrants, the latter likewise feel little connection to
established second, third, and fourth generation Koreans in Hawaiʻi. The
characters in *Guilt Payment* live in the islands yet do not interact on
significantly meaningful levels with Local Koreans precisely because
they *are* "Local," hence unable to identify with specific experiences
contributing to recent immigration to the U.S. The absence of Local
Koreans from Pak's vision of the islands indicates a view of Hawaiʻi
based primarily upon isolation and the inability to access avenues of
social interaction already established by the older generations of
Koreans. This sense of disconnection to the new land understandably
facilitates strong emotional and psychological attachments to Korea and
gives rise to the powerful role of memory in the lives of new
immigrant Koreans to Hawaiʻi.

Heart Changing Medicine

The day you arrive, silk
clings to your skin and you

refuse to remove your stockings,
which you smooth with gloved hands.
In your husband's car,
you politely endure the heat.
Back then, he refused
to turn on the air conditioning
because he thought it would waste gas,
and your back is straight while perspiration
licks away what is left of Korea.

Though he bought you a muu' muu
and flowered slippers from Woolworths,
you draw from your suitcase
a pale blue hanbok, lined silver and white.
He insists you will be too hot,
tells you this is not Korea,
but you dress silently, methodically
for your first visit.
It is your first argument.

In proper colors,
you let your steps carry you
through ginger bushes and plumeria
to what you believe will be
the merciless stare of a mother, waiting.
Instead, you are surprised
by the sound of a crying woman
whose wrinkled brown arms
stretch toward you
to grasp a memory suddenly recovered.

Tears drip down to mark
the clothes she has learned to wear
as if she can melt the distance
between then and now.
In the hot Nu'uanu rains,
an old ajumoni shakes her head
in gratitude
to the woman who has not yet taken

the heart changing medicine.

KOREAN AMERICANS: A DIASPORIC PERSPECTIVE OF IDENTITY IN *GUILT PAYMENT*

In opening his collection with the title story "Guilt Payment," Ty Pak establishes retribution and penance as themes for the stories that follow. The actions of Pak's characters in the U.S., motivated by memories of war and survival in Korea, may on the surface appear cryptic, cruel, or even cowardly. Yet given the hahn triggered by historical resonances in everyday situations, these stories illustrate the need to find peace from a new battle that translates the physical into the social, and Korea into the U.S. In addition, echoes of Korea inform characters' conceptions of identity and dismantle concepts of "nationality" based on a single nation.

"Guilt Payment" contrasts the speaker's pro-American sentiments with his daughter Mira's dissatisfaction with Hawai'i, a representation of the U.S. In belittling her father by saying, "Well, after all, it's only the University of Hawaii you are a professor at,"[19] Mira dismisses him and the U.S.—an "old country"—as backwards, passé, and limited. Such a view threatens to strip "America" of its meaning for the narrator and trivialize the reasons for his emotional investment: the horrendous events he has had to endure in order to survive and to eventually immigrate to Hawai'i. By dishonoring the past and conditions that caused her and her father to leave Korea, alluding to those circumstances only when they facilitate the manipulation of her father to get what she wants, Mira dissociates herself from the homeland. Hence, her statement "I want to show the whole world what a Korean-American can do" reflects her desire to transcend ethnic limitations (as an American who happens to be Korean) rather than her acceptance of a "Korean-American" identity based upon Korea and the influences that have brought her to the U.S.

While Mira sees Americanness as confining, especially in terms of her singing career, the speaker, like many Koreans who found themselves declared enemies of the people by the Communists, views Americans as saviors. His need for salvation is such that he neglects the fact that during the war, U.S. forces jeopardize his life as much as Communist ones: "With intensifying American air raids, which did not distinguish between military and civilian targets, it wasn't too uncommon to be reported missing, unless there were witnesses to the contrary" (8). Loyalty and gratitude to the U.S. explain the story's odd ending, in which the speaker denounces other countries in a capitalist lament of the loss of American privilege:

> I thought I had finally gotten out of all those debts, those eternal monthly salary deductions, for the car, the TV, the stereo, the piano, everything except the house mortgage, but here I go again, accepting more installment payments. Mira may indeed go on to sing at La Scalla or the Metropolitan, but even if she doesn't, well, she won't bring her mother into the picture again, at least not for a while. But why do things have to be so tough for Americans now? I remember the times when an average American income commanded princely accommodations abroad. It is quite the other way around now. Damn Arabs, damn Japanese, damn Italians, damn Koreans with their exports and favorable trade balances! (18)

By including Koreans in the list of "damn" foreigners that have turned the global economy against the U.S., the speaker demonstrates his adherence to Americanness. While he positions himself as an American, as evidenced by his verbal attack on the other countries, he also implies a desire to trade his American nationality for a Korean one, predominantly because Korea's favorable economy would help him to indulge Mira in her every whim and thus relieve his conscience over her mother's death. Nevertheless, the couching of repatriation in economic discourse only *further* Americanizes the speaker; what he longs for is not social and national reimmersion in the homeland, but the financial privilege that Americanness once represented. As it is well indicated in the story, the return to Korea is impossible: because the "wicked thing" the speaker has done to Mira's mother Yoomi took place in Korea, he cannot hope to escape it there. While he cannot forget his "crime" even in the U.S., living in Hawai'i at least affords him the luxury of American identification, a psychological severance—ineffectual though it may ultimately be—from what took place during the war.

If Americans represent deliverance for the speaker, then identifying as American permits him to construct himself as a savior and thus counter his "crime." During the Korean War, Yoomi sacrifices herself in order to save her husband and her newborn child, Mira. Watching

Mira suck at her mother's breasts like a "little vampire," endangering her mother's health by "leeching," the speaker feels "loathing" for the child, in part because he may likewise see himself as someone who lives at Yoomi's expense. While he does experience a moment of tenderness towards his child, that tenderness becomes short-lived when Mira's crying threatens to reveal their hiding place to Communist soldiers. Shortly after a failed attempt to urge Yoomi to abandon Mira, a bomb kills Yoomi and the speaker is filled with guilt and remorse. His "buying" of Mira in subsequent years—his "guilt payment"— reflects his attempt to appease his conscience. In this context, the speaker's strong affirmation of Americanness at the end of the story, as well as his conflicted feelings towards this affiliation, reflects his desire for salvation as well as his wish to become the savior. However, despite the fact that Americanness and Korean Americanness offer the possibility of redemption and escape, they ultimately recall memories of Yoomi's death and sacrifice, since it is Yoomi's death that prompts the speaker's immigration to the U.S. and gives rise to his Korean American identity.

The impact of Korea in Korean American lives is a recurrent theme in several of Pak's stories, many of which pay complex tributes to the U.S. because of America's association with salvation and survival. In "The Grateful Korean," Harry Song, another survivor of the Korean War, relives Korea's history while making his living in Hawai'i as a fisherman. During a particularly bad storm, the Coast Guard rescues him and his crew, but not without losing three of their own men. Plagued by guilt, he deeds over one longline boat each to the families of the deceased, then sells the last one to fund his children's education. Deemed "The Grateful Korean" by local and national newspapers, Harry finds himself enmeshed in an interplay of national identities that reflects Korea's history of foreign occupation, as the story becomes a metaphor for war and dominance, indicating that Korea's history transcends its geographic and periodic boundaries.

The Japanese appetite for sashimi during the New Year prompts Harry to weather a dangerous storm in order to bring in the fish. Money motivates him; also at stake is a sense of racial pride. To him, the Japanese in Hawai'i are greedy tyrants demanding satisfaction. While they never ask the fishermen to risk their lives, Harry sees this as the only way to defeat the Japanese, hence racializing his economic revenge:

> The only way to beat the Japanese middlemen at their game of price
> rigging was to turn up with a shipload of fish when the supply was
> really scarce, as during a long storm. . . . If greed had driven him,
> then at least he had put his life on the line, unlike the middlemen who
> got fat sitting in air-conditioned offices, playing golf, entertaining
> their pretty secretaries. (187)

His objection to the Japanese businessmen carries overtones of protest
to Japan's occupation of Korea and continuing exploitation of Koreans,
and in this sense, Harry has much in common with the early plantation
immigrants from Korea in his view of island Japanese. In fact, the
Japanese continue to be the enemy, interfering with the process of
Harry's American identification. Hoping to "start all over" after losing
his wife and child shortly after the Korean War, Harry immigrates to the
U.S., determined to become a self-made man. Once there, however, he
finds that the Japanese dominance in Hawai'i obstructs his business and
nearly ruins it. Harry directs his grudge towards Local Japanese rather
than the U.S., "America," or haoles for that matter, because the latter
still represent new beginnings for him. It is not surprising, then, that
in the midst of Korean-Japanese tension in Harry's business situation,
the Coast Guard occupies the same position as the American forces who
saved Koreans from the Japanese.

The conflation of economic struggles with historic and national
ones in this story paints Hawai'i as a landscape dependent upon the
memory of Korea and Harry as a man reliving Korea's history of
oppression. While this positions Harry as "Korean," Pak is careful to
emphasize Harry's liminal position between Korea and the U.S. Like
other protagonists in stories such as "Possession Sickness," "Exile,"
and "A Fire," Harry separates himself from the Korean community in
the islands. Unable to connect with his compatriots yet alienated from
the rest of Local society, Harry seeks approval and forgiveness from
haoles such as the Coast Guardsmen, the Admiral, and the families of
the deceased men. It is this impulse in Harry, and more importantly, his
successful access to the haoles in Hawai'i, that causes the other Korean
fishermen to turn against him. While jealousy has much to do with the
fishermen's hostility, Harry's rejection of the Korean community in the
islands also represents treachery connected to his desire to embrace the
U.S. and to identify as Korean *American*. In this case, connection with
other Koreans in Hawai'i implies that he has not been able to begin

anew in the U.S. or transcend his former national identity, one that carries the pain of war and loss. Less interested in diasporic integrity than integration with "America," Harry takes advantage of what he sees as the primary avenue open to him—haole approval. Only after Harry succeeds in bedding Joan Thompson, one of the Guardmen's widows, can he reestablish contact with other Koreans, because Joan assures his American identity: "The elegant, eloquent Joan Thompson stayed on for dinner and then for breakfast the next morning. That afternoon, Harry was down at Pier 17 asking about Inho Kim, Yong Ha, and Sam Chay. Were they working? Would they like to be?" (196).

That so many of Pak's main characters exist somewhere between "Korean" and "American" indicates a concern with how one "starts all over" in the U.S., though more specifically in Hawaiʻi, where AJAs (Americans of Japanese Ancestry) dominate. If entry into Local society might be considered undesirable because of its strong Japanese associations, then Pak's characters can either immerse themselves in Hawaii's Korean communities, haole communities, or, in the case of the speaker in "Exile," live in isolation, although this choice does not come without its costs.

Although "Exile" takes place well after the Korean War, many of the story's issues harken to early Korean nationalism in Hawaiʻi, and in that sense resonate strongly with the experience of Korean immigrant plantation workers. The speaker's mistrust of his church-going compatriots establishes this connection early on:

> These pastors have a ferret's instinct for rooting out their targets. I didn't have a phone and I had assiduously avoided any association with my countrymen. Not only for the usual reason of self-hatred, which is said to be very strong among Koreans. And you can't blame them, either. Korea, with its succession of incompetent, cruel, egotistic rulers, had not been much of mother to her children. Shame, revulsion, bitter disillusionment were the primary emotions she has inspired and ingrained. And so long as Syngman Rhee and his henchmen enjoyed the support of America, the country where fortune had cast me adrift, I had no more particular reasons to hide. (153)

The Korean War and Syngman Rhee's corruption thus become one in a long line of the many tragedies that have befallen Korea, and makes possible similarities in social conditions between the speaker's era and that of the early Korean immigrants. The church continues to serve as a forum for nationalist sentiments here, yet for the speaker, these sentiments are inactive and paralyzed. Feeling rejected by the U.S., the Korean parishioners meet to air their grievances against "the new country" and form the Committee for Re-Immigration to the United Fatherland. Yet as all are aware, these efforts will go nowhere:

> No Korean party was complete unless something grand was organized, to which everybody clapped and swore eternal allegiance. Of course nobody remembered a thing about it the next morning and it was bad manners even to bring it up. Deacon Cho was a well-mannered Korean and so was everybody else at Shim's. (168)

While all recognize that they will not repatriate, what separates the speaker from the rest of the parishioners is his refusal to engage in wishful return. His experiences with the corruption of post-war Korea as an anti-Rhee assassin forbid his sentimentalizing of the homeland. He refuses to take part in the Korean community in Hawai'i precisely because of its strong ties to Korea, a country closed off to him.

His sense of exile and isolation does not limit itself to Korea; neither does he permit his relationship with his Hawaiian employer, Mr. Kealoha, to affect him on little more than a utilitarian level. When Kealoha gives the speaker a piece of land to thank him for saving his life, the speaker reduces this gesture of thanks to a give-and-take transaction that almost burdens him:

> Nothing would dissuade this Hawaiian gentleman from making me this gift. He had a strain of royal blood in his veins and lived by a code of fairness unique to the native islanders. To refuse beyond what modesty required was to insult him, or worse, condemn him to the eternal vagabondage of the ingrate spirit in the nether world of Hawaiian theology. Eventually I learned to justify the acquisition as a just payment for my years of free labor. (167)

The speaker shows reluctance to incur more "debt," as debt requires connection and obligation, the exact opposite of what he desires: "Hadn't I paid my dues, those years of dodging and hiding in Korea, then the twenty years of servitude to an adipose Hawaiian?" (160). To pay his dues is to have a clean slate.

The toil and labor that the speaker puts into cultivating his land is interesting in that it invokes the "clean slate" theory and indicates a new beginning, in addition to lending itself to the notion of the "hard working immigrant."[20] Interestingly, the host in this situation is not the U.S. but a native Hawaiian; this detail resonates with the speaker's rejection of America, a country that he "had been conditioned to hate." That Kealoha gives the speaker the new start as opposed to the U.S. eases the border-crossing, since the new land is Hawaiian and not American. However, the speaker's "exile" and comfortable transition come at the expense of native dispossession: the absence of other Hawaiians in the story, especially those who are homeless or who do not own land, naturalizes Kealoha's privileged position—a construction that elides the effects of colonization upon native people.[21] While the speaker rejects Koreans in Hawaiʻi, he likewise refuses connections with Locals, haoles, or Hawaiians, and in that sense, discards all national and social identifications. He can build his "exile"/neutrality, then, only on the backs of native Hawaiians, and the implications of this dynamic ironically form a stronger association between him, his compatriots, and "America," than he might have intended; as a participant in a continuing system of colonization, the speaker gains his exile at the price of Hawaiian self-determination.

The speaker's independence, which fails to challenge systems of domination and colonization that have themselves victimized Korea and Koreans, raises the important issue of native Hawaiian absence in Local discussions. As I will assert in the next chapter, Local culture accepts Hawaiians insofar as the latter remain contained within established and nonthreatening parameters. Hawaiian sovereignty incites Local anxiety and resistance because it disrupts those parameters and demands that Locals acknowledge and take responsibility for their part in the colonization of the Hawaiian nation. A parallel here between Koreans and Hawaiians begins to surface: the politicized presence of both challenges established concepts of ethnicity, namely pan-Asian and Local identities, as well as their historical narratives. But to bring the complexity of diasporic Korean identity to the table at the expense of Hawaiian sovereignty issues only continues the hegemonic practice and indicates the degree to which the victims' minds have been colonized into replicating systems of oppression.[22]

Given that Localness has never claimed to be at odds with Americanness, as Locals undeniably assume American nationality, the protagonists' need to identify as "American" rather than "Local" in "Guilt Payment" and "The Grateful Korean" is disruptive in that it asserts a difference between the two identities. Korean historic conditions, particularly colonization by the Japanese, make Local affiliation difficult for Koreans precisely because the large Japanese population in the islands results in the equating of "Local" with "Japanese." In this sense, Korean plantation workers and post-1965 Korean immigrants find common ground in their relationships to haoles, who represent "Americans" thus "non-Locals." In the case of "Exile," "American," "Local," and "Korean" fail to describe the speaker's national connections. However, even his identity as an exile is challenged, largely because his participation in an oppressive system undermines notions of an exilic, "guilt-free" position. Resonances of Korea and the war interrogate social and institutional relationships and overthrow "stable" identities even in the "nonthreatening" climate of Hawai'i—not only in "Exile," but in Pak's other stories as well.

SITUATIONAL NATIONALITY AND IDENTITY

The shortest of Pak's stories in *Guilt Payment*, "Identity" takes place entirely in Korea. Corporal Yoon, accused of being a Communist soldier and spy, insists that despite his enlisting in the People's Army, he is "anti-Red": "'I have never been a Communist. I don't know what Communism means, except it is something I was told to hate before 1950, then to love, then hate'" (64). Although the story never reveals whether or not Yoon lies about his identity, this is less the point than the fact that the war has eradicated sources of validation, and that no one's credibility—not even the narrator's—is guaranteed:

> What if at this moment somebody should play a practical joke and recognize me as a partisan comrade-in-arms in the Chiri campaigns? Nobody saw me in Seoul during the three-month Communist occupation. My father was killed in a manner known only to his Communist captors. Mother died in Pusan at the refugee camp. . . . My brother Choo, whose face closely resembled mine, had been killed much earlier in an air raid. But didn't I have my official records, my official papers? No, the family registers and other records

had all burned to ashes during the conflagration of September 1950 as
MacArthur's Marines "neutralized" the city. There was no way to tell
my past, my identity. Any freak coincidence could disprove it all.
(66)

Especially for those who lived in areas closest to the 38th Parallel
during the Korean War, survival necessitated assuming the "correct"
identity. "The St. Peter of Seoul," "A Second Chance," and "A
Regeneration" all depict characters who both willingly and not so
willingly fight for the "other side," whether it be Communist, or U.N.
Because war disrupts and complicates stable identities, it is not
surprising that for survivors of the war, identification remains slippery
even in the "safety" of the U.S., and in some cases, even requires the
creation of an entirely new history. In "A Fire," Allen Shin, adopted as
an infant and taken to the U.S. after escaping a fire and crossing the
"heavily-mined no-man's land" that divides North and South Korea,
goes back to find his roots after the death of his patron, Major Dunbar.
Hoping that a return to his "true" origins can erase the pain and
hardship he has undergone in the U.S. as an "Oriental with a Caucasian
name," Allen wishes to begin anew, looking to the homeland rather
than the U.S. for a starting point:

> He would find his original true being, uncluttered by spurious
> additions. He went to court and had his name changed to Shin,
> which he had picked at random from a list of a few dozen. He was
> sure Dunbar would understand. It had been like matrimony in a way
> and his loyalty should not extend beyond death. He was starting
> over again, with a new identity. (100)

The war's erasure of his Korean past make his choices—from a village,
to a clan, to kinship—indeed random. Yet this kind of self-construction
can only take place in the homeland, since Dunbar has already provided
him with an identity in America.

Allen's return to Korea as an American places foreignness and the
burden of acculturation upon himself. The difficulty of such a process
eventually causes his desire for "homecoming" to fall by the wayside as
he rejects more and more of Korea, in part because "belonging" requires
the renegotiation of his American identity; eventually Allen's only
comfort comes from isolation from his adopted community.

Ultimately, Allen *cannot* satisfactorily recreate himself, as doing so requires the shedding of a displacement not easily overcome. His identities as an "American" in Korea and a "Korean" in the U.S. both lack significant emotional meaning for him, and the slippery nature of nationality feeds into a detachment that Allen translates into invincibility: "He had come through fire and hell. He had beaten all odds. He was a lucky devil. Nothing could touch him" (104). However, this invincibility is self-consuming and self-destructive, as Allen perishes in a fire during his declaration of invulnerability; Pak's choice to illustrate Allen dying by the very thing he originally survives reflects the impossibility of escaping the conditions that foster a diasporic identity.

Two stories that appear to be anomalies in Pak's collection—"The Boar" and "The Water Tower"—in fact elaborate upon situational identity. "The Boar," though in line with stories depicting military conflict in Korea, provides a dark comic-relief to Pak's other war stories. "The Water Tower," which contains no mention of the Korean War, takes place in Saudi Arabia and appears to function as a vehicle for anti-Arabian sentiments. Both stories address the issue of identity by providing backdrops of "disorder" that force their characters to adjust accordingly to their environments. The characters' success or failure thus depends upon their ability to properly read and respond to predicaments that affect self-conception and national identity.

In "The Boar," the difference between Captain Pang's and Lieutenant Nam's operations of an anti-Communist regiment manifests in a personal conflict between Nam and Private Inho Lim, a soldier highly respected by Pang. While Pang has little regard for rules and regulations, Nam lives by a concept of unwavering order that makes him unpopular with the soldiers, especially Inho, a man who in Nam's view "typifie[s] the laxity that pervaded the Third Company from top to bottom" (70). To his dismay, the other men respect and lionize Inho. This fuels Nam's rage, as well as his need to institute discipline. The Lieutenant adheres to a code of hard-work and military ethics that regards the men as little more than cogs in a machine, while Pang, whose "uniform looked as if he had slept in it," inspires the men, "who uncomplainingly worked extra long hours at the outguard foxholes, on mine-laying details and special patrols" (71). Yet for Nam, the issue is less about getting things done than doing things "the right way," particularly because for him "the right way" ensures South Korea's survival.

Wanting to make an example of Inho, Nam sabotages the soldier's opportunity to take leave for his father's birthday and present him with a boar from the hills. Because Nam sees himself as patriotic and nationalistic, hence authentically Korean, he sees Inho's wish to be among family as a traitorous attack *against* the nation, and thus defends his disciplinary actions in terms of national integrity:

> "I am an officer and you are an enlisted man. The army is a strict hierarchy, a chain of command. Everything I do is for the good of the army, for the good of the country. There is nothing personal in what I have done. It was my patriotic duty." (71)

Nam's inability to forego his conception of Korean nationality via rules and regulations becomes the very tool with which Inho defeats him. Nam finds that the disciplinary methods to be used against Inho, who physically attacks him, will only result in his own reputation as a "spineless coward" whose enlisted man beat him. Further emphasizing the absurdity of Nam's military rhetoric, Captain Pang and Inho reencode military discourse. As punishment, Pang orders Inho on duty to "capture a prisoner," and when Inho returns with a his "prisoner"—a boar—the men in the regiment treat themselves to a feast to celebrate Inho's victory.

Ironically, Nam's conception of Korean nationalism and identity results in his exclusion from and defeat by the very forces that fight to defend South Korea. Patriotism comes to center around the material realities of war rather than the abstract codes of behavior that Nam favors. His vision of national devotion, because it does not take into account disruptions and reversals caused by war and the will to survive, exists in a vacuum. Rather than provide a stable base for Korean identification, then, his rigidity destroys his identity. That he refuses to partake in the feast provided by Inho's catch, choosing instead to compose "a long letter home to explain his request for transfer" (76), only indicates his deepening isolation and his solitary sense of nationhood, neither of which contributes to Korea's independence.

In opposition to "The Boar," "The Water Tower" depicts the Korean protagonist John Bay's exploitation of a system of chaos and corruption in order to achieve his goals. The pandemonium that Bay experiences is highly problematic in that it is both racialized and nationalized: Saudi Arabia and its inhabitants become the "uncivilized" agents of lawlessness, manipulation, and immorality. The characters' anti-Arabian sentiments operate not unlike the speaker's anti-foreign statements at the end of "Guilt Payment," as both reinforce national identification. Through his racist statements, Bay affirms his American nationality, in part to distinguish himself from his fellow Korean—*not* Korean American—countrymen assigned to the contracting job on which he assists.

Bay's Korean self-hatred, witnessed by the Americanizing of his name and his vow "never to have anything to do with his compatriots" (177), contributes to his need to separate himself from the other Koreans, especially since the system in which he finds himself makes no distinction between "Korean" and "Korean American." Tago, Bay's colleague and one-time romantic rival, describes the business game in Saudi Arabia as such:

> "That's the name of the game. The Arabs are too fat and dumb to do anything themselves, so they specialize in the art of manipulating their foreign servitors by pitting one against another. They hire a Swede to draw the plans, an Englishman to supervise, and a dirt cheap Korean to do the job." (170)

The rules of the game force Bay into Korean identification, yet unlike Nam in "The Boar," Bay accepts a seemingly disruptive identity insofar as it allows him to attain his goals. However, two significant factors permit him to successfully access/exploit the Saudi Arabian system at the same time he *resists* it. First, the vehicle through which he affirms his *Americanness* (racism against Arabs) is the same vehicle through which Tago affirms his *Koreanness*, thus allowing Bay to "disguise" his pro-American rhetoric as pro-Korean solidarity. Second, that Tago must act as a cultural guide to Saudi Arabia allows Bay to assume an unfamiliarity with Saudi Arabia that contributes to his first-world self-conception. Although both Bay and Tago exist as "Korean" within Saudia Arabia, the difference between them is played out through their positions in the global economy. Bay's American economic privilege prevents him from comprehending why Koreans would work in a place they so obviously detest:

"Why take on jobs here of all places?" John asked.

Tago took a while answering the simple question, as if addressing a profound metaphysical issue.

"Because in this recession this is the only place left in the world to pick up a few dollars. Korean goods are not selling too well on the international market. All we can do is dump our labor." (171)

Thus while Tago and the others must commodify themselves as a form of "cheap imported good" to make a living, Bay's American privilege enables him to go to Saudi Arabia simply to mete out personal revenge against Tago: "He had dropped everything and flown over not so much to help as to triumph over his old friend and rival in distress" (177).[23]

Saudi Arabia, precisely because its racialized business operations give rise to the reification of national identity, provides the necessary landscape for Bay's U.S. nationalistic arrogance. While Saudi Arabia may dismiss Bay as just another "dirt cheap Korean," the Koreans he works with pay respect to him as "the great engineer from America come to deliver them from impending peril" (180), thus recalling the messianic vision of the U.S. in Korea's past political affairs. Bay's allegiance lies undeniably with the U.S., yet his nationality becomes slippery because it is his Korean past that motivates his American identification. For Bay, who had come from an impoverished but aristocratic family in Korea, Americanness offers him the opportunity to gloat over the troubles of the once wealthy and privileged Tago.[24] A variation on the notion of America as the "land of opportunity," Bay's perspective reflects the desire to affirm the American Dream ideology and testify that one *can* make it in the U.S. as well as gain first world privilege over the third world homeland. However, Bay fails to realize his continuing connection to Korea and the fact that he cannot sever himself from his past. While his memories operate as one form of connective tissue between his Korean and American nationalities, Pak further emphasizes this association through Bay's son: although Tago married Bay's former lover Ayran, the child she bore was Bay's. This information, made known to Bay only after Tago's death, prompts him to return to Saudi Arabia to help Tago's faltering company recover. In addition to rescuing Ayran from debt, Bay offers his help out of respect for Tago, shattered by the realization of his son's true paternity. Hence

Bay finds resolution in his Korean past only by accepting its continuing presence as well as its influence over his American identity. Bay's resolution is one example among many of the kinds of border-crossings that occur through women characters in Pak's stories. Women's bodies and sexualities lie at the crux of men's mobility here, and often act as catalysts for transformation, realization, and national identification. Nationalism and nationality in any context are subject to ruptures and inconsistencies that deconstruct their integrity, and women do not stabilize these conceptions in *Guilt Payment*. However, desire and sexuality provide the textual launching of many characters' access to new physical as well as social and political territories.

A "REGENERATION": WOMEN AS VEHICLES OF BORDER-CROSSING

The women in Pak's stories tend to fall into two categories: idealized saints and manipulative opportunists. Such problematic depictions support Elaine Kim's criticism that the "various manifestations of misogyny" in *Guilt Payment* compromise the vividness and excitement of Pak's action-oriented stories.[25] Nevertheless, I would like to pursue Pak's constructions of women here, as gender occupies a significant position in the discussion of Korean nationality and its relationship to Local culture. Because the predominant stereotype of Korean women in Hawai'i is that of the "bar girl," exploring the delineation of Korean women's sexualities here will further the discussion of the ways in which literature by Korean authors in Hawai'i reflects the position of Koreans within Local culture.

While "KBs" have become an integral part of Local culture,[26] this inclusion is based upon exploitation, specifically the commodification of women's sexuality. Hence the predominance of Korean bars in Hawai'i no more reflects the participation of Koreans in Local culture than the prevalence of Latina housekeepers indicates *their* entry into California's dominant society. Ostracized by both Locals and Koreans in Hawai'i, bar girls occupy a sexualized space that causes the devaluation and delegitimization of their agency and economic access. Immigration narratives, then, tend to ignore or undercut the experiences of these women, who are negatively characterized.

Some of Pak's stories concern bar girls or women who use sexuality to achieve mobility; other narratives romanticize women as martyrs. What these characters have in common, however, are their essential roles in men's border-crossings. This is not to say that Pak's women characters do not likewise use men to initiate their own cross-categorical journeys; yet when these women instigate utilitarian relationships, especially with American men, they are punished textually. Only when women remain within parameters of behavior authorized by Korean men—for instance, as mothers or dutiful lovers— do they escape criticism. This dynamic points to a strong privileging of border-crossings that involve nationally and patriarchally legitimized roles over those in resistance to a system that contains and limits women's agency. Because Pak's stories address national identity, the relationship between gender and nationality is crucial here. Koreans in Hawai'i may be outsiders to Local culture, yet the stratification within island Korean society reflects the tension between those who have "legitimately" crossed over and those who have lost their claims to Koreanness in their particular pursuits of the American Dream.

In certain contexts, the power of Korean women is indeed threatening, and it is Pak's story "Possession Sickness" that most overtly demonizes female sexual power. Although the Korean government now respects the shaman as a national treasure, Korean society traditionally considered shamans pariahs:

> In some sense a shaman was like a vestal virgin or a nun, but there was no equivalent prestige. Exactly the opposite. People might engage a shaman, fawning while they needed her, but as soon as her services were terminated, they turned around and spat at her. The shaman fulfilled a function in demand, but it was a profession even the poorest refused to go into, however financially rewarding it might be. The stigma branded and doomed not only its practitioner but also her relatives, for generations. . . . It was unthinkable that a girl from a good family with means should become a shaman. Being a shaman was in some sense worse than being dead. (26)

Representing a fate "worse than death," shamanism operates similarly to prostitution in that its use of women is denigrated yet socially institutionalized. That shaman rituals involve the female body, and that possession sickness—the method by which spirits summon shamans to their calling—can manifest itself sexually further demonstrates the connection between the two. To a large degree, to have a shaman's power is to have an amplified female sexual presence, which threatens a patriarchal order.

The battle between George Khan and his wife Moonhee over their daughter Aileen illustrates several contested sites involving gender and nationality. The shaman's powers are largely hereditary; when George Khan leaves Korea with Aileen to escape Moonhee's shamanistic influence, he wishes not only to restrain his daughter's sexuality and female power, but to save her from her birthright. In addition, Moonhee's influence, signifying Korean cultural revival, reflects a potent national identity that George wishes to abandon. Thus he plays out his cultural anxiety on Aileen, negating her Koreanness:

> "Why are you so dead set against anything Korean?" [Aileen] lashed out after a short remission. "Weren't you born and raised in Korea? Look at your name, Khan. Who would think it was Korean? What are you ashamed of or afraid of? I want to learn about Korea, learn to speak the language, learn about my ancestry. Nothing can change the fact that I have Korean blood in me. Tell me who my mother is, Father!" (20)

Ultimately, Aileen can no more resist her shamanistic calling than she can erase her national origins. Although George's surrender of Aileen to the Korean Shaman Association appears to attest to his acceptance of Koreanness, female sexuality, and spirituality, this surrender comes from fear. Having seen Moonhee undergo her possession sickness, George prefers that Aileen give in to her calling rather than fight it and risk death. Furthermore, George understands that severing Aileen from her calling comes with a price: Moonhee, likewise wishing to save Aileen from her fate, disowns her, yet dies in a plane crash as punishment for intervening with maternal protectiveness.

The narrative constructs Moonhee's maternity in colonial discourse, attributing a hegemonic power to her love for her daughter:

> Poor Moonhee, psychic yet so blind! The spirits had no other way of overcoming the intransigence of her maternal protectiveness, sincere but misguided, like the paternalism of dictators that cannot be broken except by a coup d'etat. (29)

Transforming her attachment to Aileen into a dictatorial power, this characterization reveals conflicted impulses within the narrative. While Moonhee's sacrifice can be read as the actions of a dutiful mother, the story refuses to allow her death to compensate for the threat of her shamanistic and counter-patriarchal power, precisely because of the magnitude of that power. Thus Moonhee can only express maternal love if it is characterized as corrupt and oppressive. Besides displacing traditional patriarchal qualities onto Moonhee by likening her maternal instincts to a dictator's paternalism—thus forcing the real presence of Korean institutionalized sexism into the background—this metaphor permits George to reposition himself as outside the circumstances of Moonhee's death and Aileen's calling. By the end of the story, George becomes the sole agent of Aileen's reconnection to shamanism and Korean nationality; however, his ability to do this is built upon Moonhee's death.

The presence of Moonhee's dead and tortured body becomes necessary to "Possession Sickness" in that it both allows and motivates George to undergo border-crossings: her possession sickness carries him to the U.S., while her death takes him back to Korea. In other stories, characters' nationalities likewise depend upon access to or the destruction of women's bodies. To return to some of the works previously discussed in this chapter, Yoomi's death in "Guilt Payment" inspires her husband's fervent American identification, and in turn, their daughter's desire for international/cosmopolitan recognition. John Bay in "A Water Tower" makes peace with his Korean nationality only after reclaiming his lost love Ayran, and their son. "The Grateful Korean" depicts Harry Song's integration into American/haole society through his physical intimacy with Joan Thompson, who offers him participation in U.S. global economic domination :

> "The country needs men like you to work the sea. Our seas are fished to exhaustion by other nations, while we sit back, landlocked, doing nothing. . . . Honolulu should be the base for an outreaching global fishing industry of our own. Like the whalers that used to sail the seven seas. That's why my partners and I have come up with the capital to buy more boats, to really go into fishing big. In fact, I represent substantial sums of money, millions of dollars, from many other sources. We want you to build and operate the tuna industry on a meaningful scale, first to match and then to outstrip the Japanese

and Russian pirates. How about it? Look upon it as a patriotic duty and just do it. . . . " (195-196)

Ironically, Harry's American acceptance through Joan reconnects him to his Korean nationality, redefined as strength in that Joan's proposition grants him economic revenge for Japan's and Russia's past exploitation of Korea. Furthermore, that Joan represents a reincarnation of Harry's deceased wife Moonhee links Koreanness and Americanness and emphasizes the Korean woman once again as the primary vehicle for border-crossing.

"A Fire" deals overtly with a Korean bar girl character. The narrative, strongly sympathetic to Allen's loss of Korean nationality, portrays his wife Sunhee as a "bitch" who traps Allen into marriage by faking a pregnancy in Korea and uses him to come to the U.S. After spending all his money on "clothes from Carol and Mary, jewelry at the House of Adler, furniture at Jorgenson's" (102), Sunhee becomes a bar girl, moves out of their apartment, and cleans out their checking and savings accounts while Allen is away on business.

Sunhee's actions are certainly less than commendable, yet textually, condemnation falls heavily upon her character whereas Allen escapes relatively unscathed for his own questionable actions and attitudes, such as his exploitation of and arrogance towards the Koreans with whom he seeks kinship. While one can argue that Allen simply attempts to regain what had been taken from him by the war—that is, his past—the methods by which he and Sunhee attain their respective goals do not significantly differ. Allen employs what he has (his American privilege) to access Korean nationality in the same way Sunhee utilizes the tool available to her (sexual aggressiveness) to pursue American nationality. Both characters produce narratives to facilitate the execution of their plans: Sunhee creates a pregnancy, while Allen invents the life he imagines he has lost. In addition, in the same way that Sunhee needs Allen to gain American identification, Allen needs Sunhee to solidify his Korean connection, as she provides his one link to a village of Koreans that "[annoy] him unbearably." However, the story positions Allen as the victim who is "conned" by Sunhee and thus leaves no room for the exploration of Sunhee's agency, which the narrator, because it uses sexual commodification to disrupt a system of restricted mobility for women, equates with castration:

All his plans had been shattered. There was not to be a new life. Knowing herself to be secure, now that she was on American soil, she openly scoffed at him. Did he think she would be tied down like a brood mare to start his dynasty, to make him the Adam of his race? (102)

Besides her refusal to bear Allen children, Sunhee as a bar girl earns "in one night as much as he made in a week" (103), thus compounding Allen's sense of emasculation.

The hostility with which the narrative depicts Sunhee is representative of the sentiments many Koreans have not only towards bar girls, but wives and girlfriends of American soldiers. The blurring of Korean war brides with prostitutes indicates a strong Korean class, gender, and race prejudice that sees women's sexual border-crossing as an unforgivable transgression. Yet for many women, marriage and prostitution provided an "out" if not for themselves, then for their loved ones. Even as the character of Kim No Vak in Kim Yong Ik's "Translation President" plays to the "happy hooker" stereotype, she fumes when the protagonist implies that her daughter will grow to be a prostitute like herself. Kim No Vak's sexual relationship with an American G.I. enables her to send her daughter to the U.S., the "land of Christianity,"[27] and attests to the one way in which she *can* ensure her daughter's "Christian" future. Similarly, when the protagonist in Pak's "Exile" fails to provide for the family, his sister endures name-calling and ostracism for dating an American soldier in order to feed herself and her mother. Korean women's agency in these cases is punished not only because of its class and gender implications, but because of its national betrayal. After all, these women bed *American* soldiers. Legitimacy by way of marriage has little bearing on this stigma; many Korean immigrants who came to the U.S. through sponsorship by wives of U.S. servicemen avoid calling attention to their means of entry.[28] That women use their sexualities with non-Koreans disqualifies them from "respectable" Korean society in both Korea and the U.S.

For many Koreans, the connection between U.S. servicemen's wives, girlfriends, and prostitutes, and Korean bar girls in Hawai'i comes from perceived similarities in sexual transaction. In other words, women who work in KBs for money are seen as no different than women who became involved with U.S. servicemen during the war. Establishing definitive boundaries between "respectable" Koreans and bar girls, then, island Koreans create an authenticated nationality that excludes such "undesirables." However, the high visibility of bar girls disrupts this construction and generates tension among Koreans regarding Local integration. For if Koreans are considered outsiders while bar girls possess a secured though problematic position in Local culture, then we must address the effect of KBs and bar girls, as well as the wives of U.S. servicemen, on the perception of Koreans as cultural outsiders.

As much as the racial dynamics of Hawaii's Local society complicate U.S./Asia binaries, Locals as a part of the U.S. have still been influenced by a great deal of post-war rhetoric, including that regarding Asian women:

> Fantasies of Asian femininity have been imprinted on the American male psyche for generations, thanks to three major wars in the Pacific and a constellation of U.S. military bases there. Since the 1940s, more than 200,000 Asian women have married U.S. servicemen, helping spread the G.I. gospel that Asians make "good wives."[29]

By the same token, war has also cast Asian women as prostitutes, especially since the sex trade could assure these women's economic survival. In addition, the sexual commodification of immigrant women is hardly new: Hawai'i has had a long history of prostitution[30] by Chinese, Japanese, Korean, and now Vietnamese and Thai women. Together, these factors make it easy for Locals to dismiss bar girls and servicemen's wives as Others—a form of third-world imported "goods" rather than cultural participants. This dismissal relegates them to the realm of "FOBs," thus justifying their rejection by Local culture. Unfortunately, Koreans continue to blame these women for stigmatizing Koreans. It appears, then, that there are "wrong" ways to cross borders.

If relationships between Korean women and American men represent an unacceptable form of border-crossing, then what constitutes a "legitimized" border-crossing? Certainly Pak's stories do portray idealized women who sacrifice themselves and their bodies for the sake of men's survival. The crucial difference in these stories is that these characters do not threaten the status of the Korean men around them. Regardless of the actions they take and the experiences they undergo, their sacrifices reinforce Korean patriarchal systems and ideologies. For instance, in "A Regeneration," the speaker recounts how Arin, who suffers several degrading and torturous experiences, ultimately emerges as a saint figure. As a dutiful Korean wife, she has little power to object that Osa, her Communist husband, sells her to his Russian boss to advance his own career. After her new possessor rapes her in the presence of her husband, she defects to the South—a move that might be considered traitorous albeit understandable. Yet what redeems her is the propriety of her love for and devotion to her brother-in-law, Osol. Though they are technically free to marry, both observe traditional codes of behavior that exceed the law: "They should admit their love for each other and get married. There's no a single law or man to stand between them. But they act as correct and formal as two solemn diplomats" (136).

The power of Arin's righteousness regarding Osol neutralizes the actions that would have branded her as a fallen woman. Even when Osa later pursues Arin and Osol, intending to punish them for their affair, the upright behavior of the couple disempowers him:

> [Osa's] intention had been to punish them for disgracing him, and he was surprised and disappointed to find them living in the same house observing impeccable correctitude. He had expected them to be man and wife with two or three children. He had no excuse for venting his malice. (139)

Most importantly, Arin's morality demonstrates a continuing observation of duty and loyalty to the husband who mistreated her. This, as well as her undying devotion to Osol, even risking her life to find him after their separation during the war, earns Arin her vindication because it proves her to be a "respectable" woman. Thus when an American solider rapes her and she gives birth to a child with "Negroid features," the narrative elicits sympathy for her rather than emphasizing her shame.

After Osol's suicide, owing to his physical disfigurements from war injuries, the speaker marries Arin and takes her to Hawai'i, where she recovers in the "war-free, benign climate." Even as speaker initiates this border-crossing from Korea to the U.S., Arin and her biracial child Anna come to truly signify the family's entry into American society. Arin's attack by an African American soldier resonates problematically with racialized constructions of brutality and savagery; yet ironically, the magnitude of the transgression it represents for the characters *in Korea* lends it greater power to function as a tribute to racial tolerance in Hawai'i:

> I thank God that we live in Hawaii, the literal melting pot of the races. A girl with black features would be such a scandal in that she would never lead a normal life in Korea and perhaps in some parts of America. The fact that neither Arin nor I am black attracts no particular attention here: nearly half of Anna's classmates have step-parents, often of different nationalities. (151)

The choice to distinguish between the social consequences for a biracial child in Hawai'i and those on the continent reinscribes the notion of the islands as a paradise and eradicates Local racism against African Americans. Furthermore, despite the fact that the speaker's sentiments reveal an awareness of racism on the continent, they elide that racism by constructing Hawaii's "melting pot" as a valid avenue through which the speaker and his family can access an "America" that is no different from the continental U.S. This belief then paves the way not only for the speaker's abandonment of his Korean nationality and Korean traditional values, but for his embracing of an American way of life.

> Now I am a step-father with a vengeance, but I don't agonize over it, and I have to thank the high rate of divorce in this country. Who would have thought I would be the beneficiary of divorce American-style, which I used to abhor and denounce? . . . What is the price of the low divorce rate, the so-called stability of the family-oriented Korean home but massive institutionalized adultery, especially on the part of the husband, who is considered unmasculine if he cannot boast a string of mistresses? . . . The American way of easy divorce is honest and straightforward. It's above board, a clean way of doing things. The partners involved choose to stay together. It voluntarizes and humanizes the relationship. There is no inexorable bondage of the genetically-bound biological litter. We have a community of discriminating beings reaching out for the suprabiological, the spirit, if you please. (152)

The progression from Korean to American leads to a discourse of supraraciality, in which the speaker sees Americanness as transcending the impulse for genetic (racial) preservation. Thus the U.S. becomes a country that rises above racism, even as the speaker acknowledges that Anna might have experienced difficulties in "some parts of America."

By the end of the story, Arin disappears. Having recovered from her mental breakdown, she becomes an angelic figure that literally walks off into the sunset. At this point, Anna takes over the narrative. The power of Anna's blackness enables the speaker, through his association with it, to cross national boundaries and solidify them through full identification with and loyalty to his newfound American nationality. Thus not only does Arin give birth to Anna; she continues a legacy of border-crossing through Anna, who *remasculates* the speaker by providing an American nationality that redefines and empowers his gender role:

> The very word, *kayboo*, 'step-father' in Korean, has the most unsettling connotations—emasculation, the image of a spineless good-for-nothing grafting on another man's leavings, the litter and dam. However strong my love for Arin might be, I don't think it would have survived the obloquy, the inevitable attrition over the years in a climate like Korea's where we would all be outcasts, pariahs. I am simply not that strong. In spite of my seeming independence, I am a highly social creature, who cannot live without the approval and good opinion of my fellowmen. (151)

While the speaker's conversion to an American lifestyle rings self-consciously forceful, it ultimately demonstrates the depths to which he can proclaim his Americanness, given his associations with both Arin and Anna.

PAYMENT AND DEBT: TRANSLATING NATIONALITIES

Although the majority of Pak's stories in *Guilt Payment* proclaim and affirm Americanness for their characters, they likewise call attention to the complications within "nationality" based on a single nation. "Push-pull" theories of global movement challenge the one-way directionality of immigration, and Pak's works certainly illustrate the collusion of governmental and colonial powers that resulted in the influx of Koreans to the U.S., especially after the 1965 change in Asian immigration policies. Although no immigrant group to Hawai'i (or the continent for that matter) can dispute early immigrants' connections to the homeland, the establishment of a dominant Local society diminishes the impact of these ties with each successive generation of Locals. Thus the large numbers of recent Korean immigrants in Hawai'i combined with the relatively small numbers of established island Koreans lends credibility to the problematic notion that Koreans exist outside of Local culture because they are all "newcomers" with strong homeland ties. Intense political upheaval in Korea *does* strongly infuse American and Local identification with memories of Korean history, complicating neatly defined nationalities. Yet besides revealing a prejudice against those who are new to the islands, the marginalization of Koreans attests to their dismissal because of this inability to demarcate clear boundaries between Korean, American, and Local identities.

NOTES

1. In Hawai'i, Asian Americans identify as "Oriental," a term not considered derogatory.

2. This is not to imply that immigration halted between the years of 1924 and 1965. A relatively small number of adopted children, and Korean wives and children of U.S. servicemen immigrated during the 1950s. Stigmatization and small numbers contributes to the relative invisibility of this group. See Elaine H. Kim, "Korean American Literature," in *An Interethnic Companion to Asian American Literature*, ed. King-Kok Cheung (New York: Cambridge, 1997), 156-191.

3. Although the Korean war may have played a significant role in the immigration of Koreans to the U.S. during the 1960s, many newcomers today feel that the main reason they came to the U.S. centered around their desire to elevate their individual status. See Jung Ki Kim, "Some Value Questions for Ethnic Orientation: An Ethical Perspective on Korean Immigration Motives," in *Korean Immigrants in Hawaii: A Symposium on Their Background History, Acculturation and Public Policy Issues*, ed. Myongsup Shin and Daniel B. Lee (Honolulu: Korean Immigrant Welfare Association of Hawaii and Operation Manong, College of Education, University of Hawai'i, 1978), 18-26.

4. Witness to Korea's turbulent history under Japanese, U.S., and Soviet domination, Pak lived through the Korean War before coming to the U.S. in 1965 to obtain his Ph.D. in English.

5. See Elaine H. Kim, "Home is Where the *Han* Is: A Korean American Perspective on the Los Angeles Upheavals," *Reading Rodney King/Reading Urban Uprising*, ed. Robert Gooding-Williams (New York: Routledge, 1993), 215-235.

6. While "homeland" has been used mostly to refer to countries of origin of diasporic populations, I use it here to call attention to the exile Koreans felt within their own country as subjects of Japan's imperial government.

7. See Bruce Cumings, *The Origins of the Korean War Vol. 1: Liberation and the Emergence of Separate Regimes 1945-1947* (Princeton: Princeton University Press, 1981).

8. Ki-baik Lee, *A New History of Korea*, trans. Edward W. Wagner and Edward J. Schultz (Cambridge: Harvard University Press, 1984), 380-381.

9. Jung Ki Kim, 20.

10. Ibid.

11. In contrast to Filipino immigrants, Koreans experienced a greater difficulty with the language barrier because English was used less in Korea. See Daniel S. Sanders, "Social Policies and Welfare Issues in Relation to Korean Immigrants," in *Korean Immigrants in Hawaii: A Symposium on Their Background History, Acculturation and Public Policy Issues*, ed. Myongsup Shin and Daniel B. Lee (Korean Immigrant Welfare Association of Hawaii and Operation Manong, College of Education, University of Hawai'i, 1978), 29.

12. Young Sook Kim Harvey and Soon-Hyung Chung, "The Koreans," *People and Cultures of Hawaii: A Psychocultural Profile*, eds. John F. McDermott, Jr., Wen-Shing Tseng, and Thomas W. Maretzki (Honolulu: John A. Burns School of Medicine and the University of Hawai'i Press, 1980), 143.

13. Sanders, 34.

14. Ibid., 27-35. Sanders provides an illuminating discussion on the social programs of the 1970's aimed towards assimilating Asian immigrants.

15. See Harvey and Chung; also Sarah Lee Yang, "Koreans in Hawai'i," *Social Process in Hawaii* 29 (1982): 89-94.

16. More than two-thirds of Koreans in Hawai'i married partners of another ethnicity after 1950. See Yong-ho Ch'oe, "The Early Korean

Immigrants to Hawaii: A Background History," in *Korean Immigrants in Hawaii: A Symposium on Their Background History, Acculturation and Public Policy Issues*, ed. Myongsup Shin and Daniel B. Lee (Korean Immigrant Welfare Association of Hawaii and Operation Manong, College of Education, University of Hawai'i, 1978), 14.

17. Sanders, 28.

18. Harvey and Chung, 142.

19. Ty Pak, *Guilt Payment and Other Stories* (Honolulu: University of Hawai'i Press, 1983), 5. All subsequent quoted material from Ty Pak in this chapter will be indicated by the appropriate page number/s in parentheses.

20. For a discussion of the paradigm of the amnesiac immigrant who must begin anew, see Lim, 289-311.

21. For a concise overview of Hawaiian land dispossession, see Haunani-Kay Trask, *From a Native Daughter: Colonialism and Sovereignty in Hawai'i* (Monroe, ME: Common Courage, 1993), 1-28.

22. Stephen Sumida initiates an engaging discussion of the relationship between Asian/Pacific American literatures and "postcoloniality." See Sumida, "Postcolonialism," 274-288.

23. The fact that Tago goes to Saudia Arabia for personal reasons revealed later in the story does not conflict with his assessment of Koreans' positions in the global economy here. Had Tago chosen not to go abroad, another Korean would have gone in his place. See Ty Pak, 184.

24. The theme of economic revenge enabled by American nationality likewise shows up in "Nostalgia."

25. Elaine H. Kim, "Korean American Literature," 165.

26. On his 1995 tour, Frank DeLima, whose island comedy is based upon ethnic jokes, had a wealth of material on many of Hawaii's populations. However, his Korean repertoire was noticeably brief, and the majority of his jokes took Korean bar girls as their subject.

27. Kim Yong Ik, "Translation President," *Hudson Review* 33.2 (1980): 237.

28. Elaine H. Kim, "Korean American Literature," 180.

29. Joan Walsh, "Asian Women, Caucasian Men," *Image*, 2 December 1990, 12.

30. I would like to reiterate here that Korean bar girls are not necessarily prostitutes. By raising the issue of prostitution, I simply mean to invoke a history of the sale of women's bodies and sexualities in the islands.

CHAPTER 4

"Korean Local" and "Local Korean"

Works by Gary Pak

Island in your eyes,
Paradise,
Hawaii.
—*the Brothers Cazimero*[1]

Here in Los Angeles, I have had friends ask me to accompany them to Koreatown for Korean food. A perfectly reasonable request, though I never know how to explain that depending on what restaurant we go to and what waitress we get, there is a good chance that I'll be useless as a guide or host. Although I love and often crave Korean food, I rarely go to Koreatown on my own. My inability to speak, read, or even understand Korean handicaps me. It's different when my mother's there: she does all the talking, all the work. As a child, I got so used to the ease with which we accomplished things in Korean restaurants and stores that I was shocked to find that in my later years, when I tried to do the same things without her, I might as well have been haole, or Japanese, anything except Korean.

It's always difficult to explain to others that although I identify one hundred percent Korean, that my having been a "2.5" generation kid who grew up in an English-speaking house in Hawai'i means that there are differences between "Korean Koreans" and me. It took a while for me to realize that some people had a hard time even *conceiving* of a "third generation Korean." After all, Koreans are supposed to be "new immigrants." This denial of Koreans' long-time history in the U.S. does not occur on social levels only; even in my research for this particular chapter, I have come across material that conforms to this view, material that has impressed even more strongly upon me the need to write on this subject.

The totalizing perception of Koreans as "new immigrants" exists as strongly in Hawai'i as it does on the continent. As demonstrated in previous chapters, the marginalization of Koreans from Local history and culture was the result of Korean social and political events abroad. Koreans in Hawai'i must recognize a history that gave rise to their separation from Local culture. At the same time, there is the justifiable desire for Koreans who can trace their heritage back to the plantations to claim—and for a writer such as Gary Pak, write himself into—Local history. Gary Pak's work both challenges and reinforces Local culture: he disrupts its exclusionary tendencies by asserting his own Korean Local identity, while ultimately constructing a Localness that, although more inclusive, remains intact. Nevertheless, the ruptures in Pak's work call attention to the difficulty in naturalizing "the Local" as well as the notion of paradise in the islands. This chapter, then, will focus on Local ethnic interaction as depicted in Pak's *The Watcher of Waipuna and Other Stories* through the vehicles of land rights, tourism, and plantation history. While Pak does not overtly highlight Korean ethnicity in these stories, it becomes a focal point in *A Ricepaper Airplane*, a work that claims Korean history as Local history and vice-versa. The following discussion will not concentrate on the presence or absence of Koreanness in Pak's work, but rather, analyze representations of ethnic relationships in the islands as depicted by an author of Korean descent who has demonstrated his strong identification with Local culture.

Nanakuli

Before we go,
my sister's laugh follows me
and her one comment this morning:
Punahou kids in Nanakuli,
you not going come back alive.

The day is usual—

sipping Bartles & James in Big Gulp cups,
we watch the boys surf
until the sun goes down.
Later, they push hot coals from our fire,
shoving newspaper bits,
grass, glass, even empty Bud cans
into the glow.
Someone tunes a guitar
long and slow
and we sing self-conscious to the familiar strains
Me ke aloha ku'u home o Kahalu'u[2]
And because we remember
this is our last summer together
we stay silent in the dark,
watching orange sparks crackle in the wind.

Only when we gather our things
does someone joke there were no fights today.
The drive back into town will take
the better part of an hour;
nestling deep into the back seat
of the beat-up station wagon,
we talk and wait
until we are home.

LOCALS, HAWAIIAN SOVEREIGNTY, AND RACIAL FORMATION

Among Hawai'i residents, the terms "Local" and "Hawaiian" are not interchangeable, and it is useful to begin this discussion by outlining their differences. Stephen Sumida provides a definition of "Local" in his preface to *And the View from the Shore,* and it is this definition from which I would like to start:

> Race is partly at issue—but not exactly, not truly. A "local" (meaning here a certain kind of person) is usually thought of as nonwhite, for instance, a native Hawaiian, Asian American, Samoan, or Puerto Rican; or a local may be someone historically, ethnically originating in the working classes of Hawai'i, such as a Portuguese American or

a Spanish American with a family history on the sugar plantations or the ranches of *paniolo* country. A *haole*, "foreigner" in the Hawaiian tongue and nowadays meaning Caucasian, is not usually assumed to be a local. But once he or she turns out to be a "local haole," someone brought up amongst locals in Hawai'i and who knows something about the weave of his or her own ethnicity (not "just haole" but, say, Irish, Norwegian, and English) then the usual assumptions disappear. African American locals similarly have a special place, which includes more insistently the need to be introduced by the personal histories of their families' arrival in Hawai'i (i.e., perhaps to work on the sugar plantations), their upbringing, their neighborhoods, their schools, their circles of friends and family. Most *hapa haole*, "half whites," and other kinds of racially mixed "hapas" are assumed to be local. . . . Furthermore, the term "Hawaiian" is not a synonym for "local." In Hawai'i, "Hawaiian" is commonly taken to mean "native Hawaiian" is usually reserved for that use in order to avoid ambiguity among those who speak these terms—that is, among locals. . . . Thus the term "local" does not itself denote race.[3]

While Sumida solidly delineates Localness in the islands, I would add that Localness is still very much contested. At times it can refer to those who have been born in the islands or those who have lived there for an extended period of time, regardless of race—this type of classification often centers around the ability to pick up Local behavior, attitudes, and language. At other times, "Local" excludes "haole," no matter how long the person in question may have lived in Hawai'i. Yet again, "Local" can be used to exclude not only haoles, but those of an upperclass status, those who do not live a certain lifestyle, or those who do not speak pidgin English. In any case, what remains consistent is the understanding that "Local" does *not* in itself entail native Hawaiian blood.

Differentiating between "Local" and "Hawaiian" becomes extremely important here, especially when seen as a form of resistance against tourist perceptions that label everything associated with the islands as "Hawaiian." In contrast, native Hawaiian cultural territory is considered to be so specific by islanders that, for instance, non-Hawaiians do not name their children with Hawaiian names without the blessings of a kahuna: island lore contains stories of unblessed non-native children who have died or suffered illness because of such a violation.

Regardless of the respect given to Local and Hawaiian differences, however, some Locals feel hostility towards the idea of Hawaiian sovereignty, in part because it highlights these differences in such a way that Local identity is threatened. While Sumida correctly states that race is not solely the issue in Local identity, recent developments concerning native Hawaiian rights have forced race to take a primary seat in the debate, fundamentally challenging the foundations of Local culture. If we locate Local identity's origins in the solidarity built by people of color under the plantation system,[4] then the result of this coalition becomes an identity based on race that nevertheless emphasizes panethnicity and shared economic exploitation. In other words, race determined levels of disempowerment within the plantation labor system in Hawai'i and consequently the makeup of the Local group, yet the stress lay upon the notion of a collective identity. Countering this, however, such sovereignty activists as Haunani-Kay Trask have strongly held to the separation of Hawaiians and Locals, asserting that non-Hawaiian Locals fall in the same camp as colonizing haoles:

> For nationalist Hawaiians, the constant refusal of many non-
> Natives to understand their place—that is, who and where they
> are—means their claims of equal status as Natives, or worse,
> superior status over us, are nothing but racist arrogance. The
> historical reality is that no non-Native culture can claim origins in
> Hawai'i. For example, only Hawaiians have a language whose
> words, *kaona* (multiple meanings), chants, prayers, and sounds
> relate directly to Hawai'i. We are the only people whose religion
> and hundreds of gods come from the place, Hawai'i. We are the
> only people whose material culture was based on the magnificent
> lands and waters of Hawai'i. And most crucial in today's
> destructive world, we are the only people who can claim a cultural
> way of living with the land that preserved it for millennia before
> contact with the West began to despoil our birthright. No settler
> culture can claim this.[5]

Trask's position is only one of several on the issue, and tends to be among the more militant viewpoints. It is her stance in particular that most angers Locals in Hawai'i, and it is for this reason that I find it necessary to focus on her voice and interpret Local anxiety here. Trask invalidates Local claim to the islands and calls attention to the appropriation of Hawaiian culture by non-Hawaiians. Above all, Trask's accusations deflate one of the most cherished notions of Local history and culture: that we're all in it together. Darrell Lum's introduction to *The Best of Bamboo Ridge* invokes "loco-mocos," saimin, and plate-lunches—distinctive Local cuisine found nowhere else but in Hawaiʻi. These foods, especially the plate lunch, become stand-ins for racial collectivity in the islands: "a plate lunch of curry stew poured over two scoops of rice alongside a scoop of macaroni salad and a bit of kim chee" signifies the way ethnicities have mixed in Hawaiʻi, proving that "things *are* different" in the islands. Lum also calls attention to the "sensitivity to ethnicity, the environment (in particular, that valuable commodity, the land), a sense of personal lineage and family history, and the use of the sound, the languages, and the vocabulary of island people" that mark Local literature.[6] Local sensibility as defined by Lum runs closely along the lines of what Trask claims to be specifically Hawaiian, and the similarities between the two viewpoints illustrate some of the conflict between Locals and kānaka maoli over sovereignty issues. Class as a unifying force falls by the wayside: while Lum traces Local culture to the sugar plantations and labor strikes, sovereignty activists maintain that the issues go beyond that to colonialism and stolen land.

All of this points to a radical redefinition of Local identity via the "new" concept of Hawaiian racial difference. In the case of sovereignty, political power for Hawaiians relies upon the establishment of the kānaka maoli as a separate and distinct *racial* group.[7] Such a move has strong repercussions when it comes to Local identity precisely because a changing Hawaiian racial identity destabilizes other racial groups that have heretofore maintained specific relationships to "Hawaiianness." Omi and Winant elaborate upon the socially constructed nature of race, insofar as racial categorizing has been historically fluid:

> The effort must be made to understand race as an unstable and "decentered" complex of social meanings constantly being transformed by political struggle. . . . *[R]ace is a concept which signifies and symbolizes social conflicts and interests by referring to different types of human bodies.* Although the concept of race invokes biologically based human characteristics (so-called "phenotypes"), selection of these particular human features

for purposes of racial signification is always and necessarily a social and historical process.[8]

It is not surprising that in reaction to this shift, some Locals reassert Localness, thus sacrificing the specificity of Hawaiian "race," history, and culture. The phrase "Hawaiian at heart" has become especially loaded in this debate, as it seeks to legitimize a Local claim to Hawaiian land and history that assumes equality between non-Hawaiian Locals and the kānaka maoli. The notion of being "Hawaiian at heart" often lies behind the hostility some Locals harbor against outside investing by multinational corporations, and more specifically, Japanese nationals.[9] In short, attacking foreign investors reinforces Local land claims. Furthermore, the "borderless world" that multinational and transnational corporations seek to establish *grants* Locals the opportunity to resist:[10]

> [C]ulture can serve as one of the primary means of identification through which diverse inhabitants (largely Asian and Pacific in makeup) of this multiplex region have sought to resist ingestion into a global fantasy by an assertion of historical experiences and local enclaves of resistance, survival, and colonial critique. To describe myriad practices of the Asia/Pacific as "local," within contexts of transnational capital that would bypass, warp, or integrate them, is not to trivialize or parochialize them but to underscore their historicity and their strategic necessity at this time. Heteroglossic spatiality, as in Hawaii, can threaten the hegemonic modernity of the nation-state.[11]

Local resistance is certainly understandable in this regard, yet the conflict between a Local and Hawaiian nation nevertheless appears irreconcilable,[12] since the position the "Local nation" has assigned to Hawaiians *contains* the kānaka maoli in ways at odds with the goals of Hawaiian sovereignty.

Those who staunchly defend Local culture in response to sovereignty issues often work under the assumption that Localness functions as a type of ethnicity paradigm, albeit one confined to a certain historical period. Plantation laborers arriving in Hawai'i between the 1840s and the early part of the twentieth century form and conform to Local culture and establish Local history; this includes native

Hawaiians, with the understanding that native Hawaiians, while providing a base for Localness, also conformed to a culture shaped largely by Asian immigrants. Because a politicized Local identity necessitates a heritage in Hawai'i originating in the plantations, it excludes newly arrived immigrants, who are consequently labeled as "FOB." Hence the "assimilation" experience becomes historically circumscribed. When sovereignty activists assert a history and identity apart from Locals, they force a rewriting of this paradigm, emphasizing that despite the circumstances of contract labor, Locals have little or less claim to the 'āina because they occupy land stolen from the Hawaiian nation. This forces Locals to identify as oppressors, complicating a working-class consciousness and a history of economic oppression under haole plantation owners.

One dimension of Local resistance to sovereignty lies in its professing of racial harmony. If we can recognize systems of oppression in the islands that run counter to this idea, Locals may come to a different understanding of sovereignty, one that may work in collaboration with rather than in opposition to the issue. This task is indeed challenging, for many aspects of Local culture protect the concept of racial harmony and the idea that, while the land and economy may be suffering from overuse and tourism, at least we all get along.[13] For instance, the popularity of comedians such as Frank DeLima is fueled by the belief that racial jokes bring everyone down to the same level, affirming that we are in fact equal. Those who question this method of racial harmonizing are often seen as not "getting it"; more appealing are theories that claim racial jokes in Hawai'i have had a beneficial effect, equalizing the various ethnic groups:

> At its best, local comedy is an expression of local democracy. The comic's targets are arrogance and imposition; he ridicules any person or group that places itself above others or flaunts its privileges or position.
>
> The comic uses ethnic jokes to prevent any ethnic group from developing a master race mentality. . . . [W]hen taken merely as jokes, they seem to be healthy reminders that no ethnic group is perfect.[14]

Yet what happens once one leaves the show? The realities of a racial hierarchy are tangible and material in Hawai'i, from the large numbers of Filipina/os and Hawaiians in the service sector of the tourist industry, to the proliferation of Korean and Vietnamese bars and bar girls, to the overwhelming influence and presence of AJAs in island politics and economy. Given this, it is difficult to deny that Hawai'i is not the model of multicultural success for other cities in the U.S.

Gary Pak's work illustrates the tension between appreciating Hawaii's *difference*—for as much as Hawai'i strays from the idea of a multicultural paradise, there is nevertheless a racial climate there that differs from the continent—and illuminating Hawaii's dark legacy of colonialism. It is his Local "sensibility" and examination of Local culture that mark him as a "Local writer." While this appears to come at the cost of highlighting Korean ethnicity in his stories, it ultimately enables the assertion of his racial identity, thereby securing a place for it within the parameters of Local history and culture.

LAND AND HISTORICIZATION IN *THE WATCHER OF WAIPUNA*

In the 1970s, the Local renaissance took as its adversary images of Hawai'i as a tourist paradise. Writers focused on the rebirth of cultural histories, which countered perceptions of an ahistorical haven or a pleasure fantasy for travelers.[15] These cultural histories necessitated contextualization and historicization in reading Local literature; to interpret the texts otherwise risked reification of the very approaches to the islands that Local writers resisted. A contemporary Local text such as Gary Pak's *The Watcher of Waipuna* likewise requires cultural contextualization, which prevents readers from becoming "literary tourists." In the stories that comprise this collection, Pak disrupts perceptions of Hawai'i as an isolated paradise not only by demanding this contextualization, but by invoking nationhood as well as Hawaii's global connections.

Pak addresses issues of land ownership, and in the opening story, "The Valley of the Dead Air," he highlights interactions between Locals who realize that they occupy stolen land. When the kahuna Jacob Hookano dies, a hauna pervades the valley. The residents immediately connect the smell to Jacob, yet cannot pinpoint the source of his anger. When the community gathers together, it learns that Jacob's family owned all the valley land until the Cox family seized it. Earl Fritzhugh's response may echo those of the reader who fails to historicize this situation or recognize the magnitude of the crime: "'But what got to do with us? I not responsible. Dah haole wen do it. Not me.'"[16] Others insist, "I nevah bother him" and "I nevah had no problems with old Jacob." Yet this is precisely the problem, as Mineda points out: by ignoring Jacob and not "bothering" him, the residents have not only ostracized him, but failed to see their rightful relationship to him as occupants of his land. In short, they have failed to understand the history of the land on which they live.

For this reason, the community's identification with Jacob becomes morally necessary. When a haole salesman systematically dupes each family in the valley into buying expensive air freshener units and fire prevention systems that never arrive, a sense of violation and betrayal is extended to all. Shortly after this episode, the community reassesses its relationship to Jacob. Through confessions and offerings, the residents unite with Jacob at its center. The narrative suggests that this act pacifies Jacob, who seeks respect rather than punishment or relinquishment of the land. Significantly, Tats Sugimura, the one person who showed kindness to Jacob, is the only member of the community who becomes immune to the smell while his neighbors suffer.

Candace Fujikane argues that the community's confessions of various transgressions involving Jacob

> enable the community to articulate and distance itself from the painful awareness that the land upon which it bases its cultural consciousness as "Local" is stolen property. In fact, the community is freed from guilt since no one will inherit Jacob's remaining land. . . . That the smell miraculously disappears following reparations made of substituted offerings—not of land, but of food—suggests that the narrative is a purely fantasmatic one. . . . The Locals, after all, are never explicitly forced to answer the question of how they will address their position on what was once Hookano's land.[17]

Indeed, "The Valley of the Dead Air" depicts tensions between Locals and the kānaka maoli over land; however, I would argue that it remains unclear whether all is truly resolved by the end of the story, and whether the community *is* "freed from guilt." Although Jacob does die early on, his spirit returns as a very real presence, a material reminder that all has not been forgotten with his death. This testifies to the continuing issues of land rights and sovereignty in Hawai'i, issues that refuse to disappear over time. Jacob remains a force with which to reckon; although Leilani Vargas' talking back to Jacob's ghost comforts everyone momentarily, the residents nevertheless further pacify the kahuna by celebrating "in the memory of old Jacob." By the time the smell disappears and rain falls at the end of the story, all appears well, yet the presence of other Hawaiian characters in the story additionally precludes any neat outcomes here. While Earl Fritzhugh and Leimomi Vargas are themselves part-Hawaiian, they do not identify with Jacob in his loss of land. However, their presence complicates the notion that the injustice of stolen land dies with Jacob because this reading locates dispossession in the body of only one man when in fact, Vargas and Fritzhugh have likewise been affected by a system of colonialism. Vargas' and Fritzhugh's emotional distance from the crime indicates that their Hawaiian identities have been to a large degree subsumed by Local ones, yet it does not imply that the claim has disappeared or that Locals may forget their participation in the colonization of native Hawaiians.

In "A Toast to Rosita," Pak uses issues of sexuality and class to further investigate native Hawaiian dispossession. Like the Hookanos, the Kamali'i family once owned a large portion of land, though they lose it to the gambling debts of Rosita's hapa haole father rather than land taxation. The narrator tells us that, when first moving into the neighborhood, his parents felt uncomfortable in the midst of an ali'i house. Yet feelings of respect quickly gave way to a sense of personal injury when the ali'i descendents snubbed them:

> At first, our parents regarded the Kamali'i family as a sacred historical representative from our not-so-distant but cloudy past. But when Mrs. Kamali'i refused to come out of her house and associate with us, our parents began to despise them. As our father finally said, "Who dah hell dey t'ink dey are, t'inking dey bettah than us!" (W 115)

The Hawaiian hierarchical system is acceptable for the narrator's parents if it remains a part of the sacred and dead past; yet the *continuing* presence of this "cloudy past" prevents its erasure and results in social injury for non-natives. By exercising her class status over others, Mrs.

Kamali'i disrupts the Local neighbors' perceptions of Hawaiian society as something long-gone and impotent. Because the neighbors resent the Kamali'i royalty, Rosita's homosexuality serves as a convenient scapegoat for their frustrations. The community views Rosita's sexual preference as reason enough to shun him, yet in conjunction with his ali'i blood, it counters his privileged position. In this sense, Rosita is twice-disempowered: first as a member of the ruling class that can no longer rule, and second, as a mahu at the bottom of the social hierarchy. Rosita's sexuality provides an avenue through which the neighbors can undermine ali'i privilege, and they empower themselves through their disgust for Rosita's activities. When a group of fathers gathers together, the subject of Rosita strengthens and affirms their own masculinity and power:

> "Dose fricken mahus!" our father said. "Dey bettah get deah act together and get outta dis place."
> "No joke," another father said. "I no like 'em around my kids."
> "Dey bettah bag or I going break deah asses."
> "Eh Mo," one of the other fathers said playfully in a strained feminine voice. "Maybe dey like you do dat."
> The fathers broke out laughing. One of them dropped his can and beer spilled out, making a thick foamy circle. (W 119)

The implied sexual contact between Mo and "dose fricken mahus" links sex with violence in a way that metaphorically recalls the colonization of the Hawaiian nation by foreigners: these men wish to remove Rosita from the land and force him into submission through his figurative rape. As in "The Valley of the Dead Air," Locals take part in the overthrow of the Hawaiian nation and are likened to colonizing "haole" outsiders.[18]

However, their sense of power is disrupted by the State's decision to build a freeway through the neighborhood, demonstrating the difficulty in equating "Local" with "oppressor." Construction threatens the families with the loss of their homes, and, like those in "The Valley of the Dead Air," they are forced to identify with native Hawaiian dispossession. The narrator's father and the others begrudgingly sign Rosita's petition to stop the government's action, yet no one joins him in the demonstration at the State Capitol. When the lack of response forces Rosita to take more drastic measures by chaining himself to the doors of the Capitol, the narrator's father exclaims, "'Look how crazy he is. If he so concern about dis t'ing, why he no go do it dah right way?'" (W 125). The narrator's father sees Rosita's lack of legitimacy, his perceived inability to do things the "right way," as directly linked to his being māhū. The parallel between Rosita's feminization/castration—based on the reading of homosexuality as castration in homophobic perception—and the neighborhood's rape by the State is too powerful an identification for the narrator's father. His homophobia paralyzes him and prevents him from taking action against the State, ironically turning him into a passive victim, the very thing against which he defines himself. Rosita, who receives no support from his neighbors, loses his job as a result of his protest and overdoses on Valium in a fit of hopeless depression.

The living element of Hawaiian activism ends dismally in the story, yet Pak closes on a hopeful note, emphasizing the legacy of Rosita's efforts. The neighborhood children mourn Rosita, and go to his house to honor him with a toast:

> We liked Rosita; and though we didn't care too much about his being a mahu, watching his life and realizing that he had given a part of himself to us made us feel that he was one of our best friends. (W 126)

The children separate their homophobia from Rosita's efforts to save the neighborhood, something their parents fail to do.[19] Furthermore, Rosita leaves them with a sense of empowerment: through Rosita's insistence that they sign the petition and "understand what is what," they foresee their own agency and their potential to effect change:

> We studied the petition, half-filled with names, our eyes wide with excitement; the fresh signatures of our parents were on the bottom of the list. Then, in turn, we grasped the pencil firmly and wrote down our names. When we finished, we looked proudly at our tiny markings, and it felt as though we had suddenly grown taller and stronger, that part of the world now rested on our shoulders. It was a powerful feeling. (W 123)

The story maintains differences between the children's battle for land preservation and Rosita's, however. Like Jacob's ghostly laughter in "The Valley of the Dead Air," the slamming of the koa wood doors signifies an acceptance of the offering; at the same time, it causes the children to "race down the street, all the while thinking that a cold hand of the unknown was ready to snatch [them] from behind" (W 126). The threat implicit in Rosita's ghostly appearance reminds the children that they are trespassers on his property and consequently, his land. And while they may sympathize with and fight for the cause, they must remember their positions in relation to the kānaka maoli.

If Pak's stories resist "touristic" readings, we must examine where tourism and tourists *are* in his works. In one particular scene of "A Toast to Rosita," Rosita, preparing for the protest, leans against a statue of Father Damien while "on the other side of the plaza, some haole tourists were posing for a group picture" (W 124). The contrast between the tourists' landscape, in which the State Capitol serves as background for a snapshot, and Rosita's, in which the Capitol possesses the power to devastate lives, is a potent one—the difference between the view of "paradise" and "the view from the shore."[20] In island culture, "history and place are not simply two separate elements of a worldview or of a sensibility in Hawaiʻi . . . place is conceived as history—that is, as the story enacted on any given place."[21] Thus for Rosita, the Capitol is not an empty signifier, but one that recalls a history of oppression. Tourism, on the other hand, which seeks to dehistoricize, explains the tourists' ability to use the Capitol as scenery.[22] In a story addressing tourism such as "The Watcher of Waipuna," then, the fight is on one level against the greed of Gilbert's sisters as well as the development of the land for tourist usage. Yet on another level, the battle is against the erasure of stories connected to the land: those denied by the developers and forgotten by Lola and Lucy in their greed. Pak employs a collage of narratives in this story—Local, national, and native—that works to preserve the land, thereby proposing an effective alliance between Locals and Hawaiians.

The narrative that threatens Gilbert and Waipuna is typical of discovery narratives that place the genesis of a land or culture in the arrival of its colonizers. As far as Waipuna's past in concerned, all that the haole and Japanese businessmen know is that "seventy-six acres of undeveloped land had been purchased by Hawaii International Corporation, the parent company of the Honolulu businessmen, thirteen years ago for a song" (W 23). The history of Gilbert's land in particular is that it has stood in the way of a major development project: a world-class hotel resort. The businessmen's interest in Waipuna constructs its existence, and the absence of this interest marks it as ahistorical, simply lying in wait. In contrast, Pak historicizes Waipuna via the life of Gilbert Sanchez: he infuses the land with stories of Gilbert's job as a busdriver, his failed love affair, his devotion to his aging parents, and his madness. Because the land represents Gilbert's personal history and is given meaning only through his memories, it has little monetary value for him. For his sisters, however, the businessmen's seductive offer of $150,000 per acre promptly overshadows the Sanchez family history. As a result, Lola and Lucy validate the developers' narratives and pare down their family history to find the one story that will allow them to take over the Waipuna estate: that of Gilbert's madness.

Because of the strong connection between the land and the 'ohana, Lola, in selling off the property, must separate herself from the family by disclaiming Gilbert: "I no care if he's our bruddah" (W 62). In an exchange with Lucy, she likewise rewrites her relationship with her parents in attempts to concretize her distance from them. This eventually divides Lola and Lucy. While Lola dismisses her parents by creating a narrative of their "madness," Lucy feels such a move is traitorous:

> "What you mean dey wasn't in dey right mind?" Lucy returned, a bit piqued. "I could understand dem. Dey was making sense. Nothin' was wrong wit' what dey was saying."
>
> "What I mean by dat is dat Mama and Papa nevah was thinking 'bout us. We dey children, too. So we get the right to the property, too."
>
> "I still think dey was thinkin' all right. You callin' Mama and Papa stupid?"
>
> "No-no-no," Lola rattled, a bit concerned now that she was losing control of the conversation. "I nevah mean it like dat. No-no-no. I never said Mama and Papa was crazy. I jus' mean dat was hard to understand dem. You know, ever since Papa got his stroke, and den Mama right after, been hard to understand what dey sayin'."
>
> "But Gilbert always could understand. I could understand."

"I could, too," Lola rebutted. "I could understand dem."

"But how come you said you couldn't understand dem, den?"

"You don't know what I mean. What I mean is dat sometimes it was hard fo' understand dem. Plus, getting back to my original point, dey really wasn't thinkin' about us, you and me, and our families." (W 63-64)

Lola's erasure of the land's history through her betrayal of the 'ohana causes her to identify with both developers and tourists, and her discomfort with Gilbert's reminder, "Dis yo house, too" (W 47) attests to her newly acquired "outsider" position. It becomes fitting that the lawyers use her to acquire the land, as she provides the avenue through which Waipuna can become a world-class tourist resort by embodying the loss of the land's history.

As Lola's and Lucy's greed is tied to their dehistoricizing of the land, it follows that they must *rehistoricize* the land in order to rehabilitate their relationship with Gilbert and preserve the 'ohana. While Lola wholeheartedly persists in her campaign to declare Gilbert unfit and sell the estate, Lucy experiences a change of heart, significantly during a moment in which she remembers her childhood on the land:

> He approached them with the bucket. Curious, the sisters looked in, but their faces turned to disgust at the sight of half a dozen, suffocating eyeless mullets.
>
> "Agh, Gilbert! Whas wrong wit' dis fish?" Lola snapped. "What happened to dah eyes?"
>
> "Dey no mo' eyes, dis kine mullet," Gilbert explained. "I caught dem in dis hole I wen dig right down the road. Daddy wen show me how when I was small-kid time. You nevah know had all dese big limestone caves underground?"
>
> "I knew dat," Lucy answered softly. She remembered the time when as a child playing on a the roadside the ground under her had caved in, the hole taking her up to the armpits; luckily, her cries of help were heard by her father. She shuddered, thinking that slimy blind mullets could have been nibbling at her toes. (W 31)

Recalling her literal engulfment by the land, Lucy comes to see Waipuna as a part of herself and a testament to her own history. Joining forces with Gilbert against the developers and Lola, Lucy views the fight to preserve the 'āina and the fight to keep the family together as one.

While a key factor in saving Waipuna is the 'ohana, Pak constructs a similarly powerful force in the alliance between Gilbert and old man Nakakura, considered "half-crazy" because he talks "all day long about the frogmen who had come to Waipuna from the ocean during the War and were now hiding in the dense mangrove forest along the coast" (W 21). Nakakura cannot view the land apart from this remembered history; for him, Waipuna exists eternally as a landscape of war. In addition to functioning as a parable for foreign invasion, Nakakura's story invokes notions of treachery from within and betrayal by those one attempts to defend by harkening to an era of fear that manifested in Japanese American internment as well as theories of Japanese espionage. While the U.S. did not implement mass internment in Hawai'i as it did on the continent, internment *was* a very real threat and phenomenon in the islands,[23] and Nakakura's madness can also be read as psychological damage from that trauma.[24] Gary Okihiro details a report by the U.S. government emphasizing the threat of Hawaii's Japanese. This report professed that

> Japanese naval vessels anchored in Hawaiian waters to display Japan's strength and to remind those in the territory that they were Japanese. For the Japanese government . . . naval visits served the dual purpose of advancing Japanese nationalism and collecting intelligence information. The [Summerall] report alleged several instances of spying by Japanese naval officers and crew members while on shore leave; some of them disappeared into the local Japanese community and later found employment in various federal and territorial offices such as the court system, immigration service, tax office, school system, and city police.[25]

It is difficult to determine whether Nakakura truly sees Japan or the U.S. as the enemy, yet perhaps this is less the point than his need to protect Waipuna from those who wish to profit by its takeover. By leaving the nationality of the frogmen ambiguous, Pak creates space for a dual critique; significantly, the investors are both American and Japanese. Hence Nakakura imparts a specifically Local territoriality that sees both as equally detrimental.

Through the friendship of Nakakura and Gilbert, Pak constructs an active coalition between Locals and Hawaiians,[26] yet we should not read this as simply a case of the two uniting for a common purpose. Considered pupule and outcasts from the community at Waipuna, Nakakura and Gilbert function as problematic "representatives." To understand the nature of their alliance, we must look at what bonds the two and enables them to save Waipuna: madness originating in experiences with the military, a presence that recalls Hawaii's long history as an occupied territory.[27] By linking Nakakura and Gilbert through this, Pak suggests that a united effort can only be reached through remembering a politicized island history that has oppressed Locals as well as Hawaiians.[28] Thus Local ties to the land become valid weapons used to preserve the 'āina, rather than detractors from native Hawaiian rights. Furthermore, Pak's decision to militarize a story primarily about tourist development emphasizes the collusion of both industries to exploit the islands. Rob Wilson points out that the "South Pacific" fantasy, still prominent today, lay in what he calls "militourism," as Hollywood "cooperated with mass tourism and the U.S. Department of Defense to coproduce and spectacularly install a 'concrete fantasy' of a defanged American Pacific" in the 1950s that "conjured Pacific space into a white settler's paradise of animistic enchantment, technicolor racial harmony, and (to be sure) military necessity."[29] It is entirely in keeping that in Pak's story, the battle against tourist development becomes a war against foreign occupation,[30] and that Nakakura's story facilitates Gilbert's understanding of the developers' plans by translating the situation into a battle with invaders in the guise of slick businessmen.

Nakakura and Gilbert's alliance likewise fosters the combining of their historical narratives, which provide a plan of attack by allowing history to activate itself against the developers:

> So Gilbert told his plan, about how he and Lucy would have to dig into the underground limestone caves. Then they would have to wait in hiding under the bridge until the frogmen passed over them, whereupon they would come out and attack the frogmen with their sticks and chase them toward the holes. Falling into the limestone caves, the frogmen would be eaten by the blind mullets, thus getting rid of them once and for all. (W 75)

Although the plan is never implemented, the 'āina becomes an active player in the battle: the limestone caves, refusing to hold the weight of the trucks, swallow the equipment whole, eventually causing Hawaii International Corporation to declare bankruptcy. True to the connection between place and history, the "four-and-a-half acres of cleared land" (W 85) thereafter testifies to the ill-fated attempt to develop Waipuna, as well as to Lola's betrayal of Gilbert and the 'ohana. Pak's resolution to the story, however, is far from tidy. Long after Hawaii International Corporation abandons its project, Gilbert sets into a panic when he returns home to "a yard full of small frogs." For fear "that history might repeat itself" (W 86), Gilbert, the new Watcher of Waipuna, runs "like a madman" to warn the others in the village of the frogmen's return. The war continues, and although Gilbert succeeds in keeping his land, the threat of its takeover does not subside.

In addition, as a collaboration of narratives rather than a collection of individual stories, *The Watcher of Waipuna* questions perceptions of racial harmony. Coalition between Hawaiians and Locals does not indicate the erasure of racial tension in Hawai'i. Although after his death Nakakura joins the ranks of what appears to be Night Marchers,[31] perhaps signaling his union with Hawaiians, we cannot assume that the history or presence of racism has been eradicated, and the inclusion of a story such as "The Trial of Goro Fukushima" attests to this.

"The Trial of Goro Fukushima," exploring anti-Japanese sentiment during the plantation era, is based upon the real-life lynching of Hiroshi Goto in 1889:[32]

> On October 28, 1889, the trussed-up body of Hiroshi Goto, a storekeeper and well-known advocate of Japanese workers in the Honokaa area of the island of Hawaii, was found hanging from a telephone pole. The news spread quickly within the Japanese community. Many believed that Goto's lynching was instigated by the planters because of his outspoken defense of Japanese workers in court. Five "foreigners"—*lunas* on a nearby plantation—and a "Hawaiian" were charged with manslaughter. The five whites were found guilty of manslaughter but were released on bail pending an appeal; they promptly vanished from the islands.[33]

In contrast to Goto, however, Goro Fukushima is a gardener who speaks very little English, and whose concerns revolve not around the "defense of Japanese workers" but his job as a gardener for the church and the Lazarus family. While Goto's outspokenness posed a threat to the haole lunas, Fukushima chooses to live his life away from the Japanese camp as a quiet loner. Fukushima's death simply results from his being in the wrong place at the wrong time: his well-meaning attempts to help Mrs. Lazarus after her botched abortion only implicate him as an adulterer and murderer in the eyes of the lunas. The fact that two such different men as Goto and Fukushima suffer the same fate is exactly the point here: racism and acts of violence do not only target those who challenge the prevailing power structure. Because the plantation system in Hawai'i depended upon its laborers' expendability, and labor strategy involved working each group to exhaustion for maximum production and replacing the exhausted group with a new group of ethnic laborers, anti-Japanese sentiment became part and parcel of the islands' economic system, especially since the Japanese were the dominant group:

> The exploitation of Hawaii's natural resources of sandalwood and whales was succeeded by the exploitation of laborers—Hawaiians, Chinese, Japanese, Filipinos, and smaller numbers of Portuguese, Spaniards, Russians, and Norwegians—within a plantation system that voraciously consumed workers like crushed cane. The crushing of Japanese migrants, herein presented as Hawaii's anti-Japanese movement, was systematic and endemic to capitalism in Hawaii.[34]

Pak's story depicts neither Fukushima nor his ally Kazuo Iwamoto as a plantation worker, yet this only strengthens his illustration of racism by demonstrating the breadth of the oppressive order: racism is not confined to the plantations.

That nearly all in the multiethnic community believe Fukushima guilty of adultery and murder reflects the degree to which anti-Japanese sentiment has been internalized, as well as the lengths to which the community will go to preserve itself. If the others attribute Fukushima's lynching to the gardener's "crime" rather than the racism of the plantation owners and lunas, it follows that they do not acknowledge the ways in which *they* are exploited by the haole owners.

Their willingness to sacrifice Fukushima disrupts a simplistic view of Local ethnic cohesion by indicating that solidarity between Fukushima and the others is tenuous if not nonexistent. For example, despite the fact that Maria Texeira is, like Fukushima, utilized and mistreated by the Lazarus family, she nevertheless sides with the church and the Lazaruses in condemning Fukushima. The fact she, like the Japanese laborers, eats dandelion weeds to stave off hunger, marking her as what Sau-ling Wong would term a "champion eater"—one who must by "necessity" espouse "efficient eating"[35]—serves as no sign of their shared oppression. Texeira thinks of her dandelion-eating only in contrast to the meat-eating Lazaruses; she consciously separates her status as "less" from Fukushima's, thereby creating another tier in the hierarchy by which she is superior to the Japanese gardener.

The community's quickness to condemn Fukushima also reflects the deference of the community to the power of the church, and their deification of the Father:

> There was little doubt in the minds of the congregation that the Japanese gardener, Goro Fukushima, had murdered the wife of the plantation manager. After all, if the Father said that Goro Fukushima had committed that sin, then God was surely the witness to the murder. (W 98)

As Pak himself notes, the church functions as a "unifying force,"[36] albeit one that has dangerous and deadly consequences. Although the Father is clearly implicated in Fukushima's lynching through his own sin and hypocrisy, Pak's narrative resists the view that missionaries brought corruption to what would otherwise be a peaceful civilization. Pak's story certainly illustrates an abuse of power, yet he is careful not to invoke an idyllic past or to position Hawaiians as historically unidimensional victims lacking agency. Johnny Kealoha's complicity in the crimes of adultery and lynching is enough to signify that the situation is complex, not simply a case of the colonizers versus the colonized. Furthermore, Mrs. Lazarus' Hawaiian blood complicates a strict correlation between race and power, proving it difficult to associate privilege with whiteness only. At the same time the story is entirely about race, it also refuses to comply with uninterrogated racial categorizations, and once again challenges any ahistorical or reductive readings of Hawaii's history and people.

In *The Watcher of Waipuna,* Pak displays various facets of Local culture and history. Narratives of historical injustice and racism prevent his collection from endorsing Hawaiʻi as a paradise abstracted from history, and for one to walk away from *The Watcher of Waipuna* with that conclusion is to dismiss and ignore the ways Pak's stories take issue with touristic readings of Hawaii's literature. Yet as much as the presence of racism in his collection points to ruptures in the myth of Hawaii's "mixed plate," the conspicuous absence of Koreans from most of his stories likewise indicates that not everyone enjoys equal representation. In answer to this, Pak's novel, *A Ricepaper Airplane,* takes as its subject Korean immigration, plantation experiences, and nationalism, all in the context of Local history, and speaks to the need for voicing a specifically "Local Korean" identity.

LOCATING "LOCAL KOREANS": *A RICEPAPER AIRPLANE*

Certainly Gary Pak is not the only Korean from Hawaiʻi to have contributed to the body of island literature. Yet when we speak of a Local "sensibility," Pak represents Localness in ways that other Korean writers from Hawaiʻi have not. His work displays easily recognizable signs of Local culture; the stories in *The Watcher of Waipuna* resonate strongly with Local readers because they reflect what we see as island life. While these stories question Local society's cohesiveness, they do not challenge its racial perceptions by insisting that Local Korean invisibility be accounted for.

Yet precisely because Pak's work has established his reputation as a Local writer, it has laid the groundwork for a project that seeks to write Koreans both historically and contemporaneously into Local culture. *A Ricepaper Airplane* recounts the story of a Korean immigrant, Kim Sung Wha, who sails to Hawaiʻi in the 1920s in order to escape the Japanese government. While Kim fights to survive both on the plantations and off, his wish to return to Korea and reunite with his wife and child motivates him to build a plane with ricepaper wings. Told through a complex narrative that employs stream of consciousness writing as well as shifts in time and speakers, *A Ricepaper Airplane* contests linearity that excludes: Pak's project seeks nothing less than the writing of Koreans into the weave of Local history.

Given the relative lack of academic and literary recognition regarding the Korean plantation experience in Hawaiʻi, Pak's narrative is both subversive and revolutionary. Many historians who have mentioned Korean plantation laborers have done so in connection to strikebreaking, thus constructing Koreans as those upholding the oppressive order. What these historians gloss over, however, is the impetus behind such a move. In the year following the 1919 Mansei demonstration in Korea, Koreans in Hawai'i were eager to thwart the Japanese in any way possible, including the attempt to render ineffective what has been called the first multiethnic strike in U.S. history. Pak's treatment of the strike in *A Ricepaper Airplane* allows Korean resistance to be embodied by living, breathing agents; at the same time, Pak frustrates the circumscription of Koreans as single-mindedly nationalistic and anti-Japanese by presenting Sung Wha's dissident viewpoint that he and the others are wrong to strikebreak. One might argue that Pak's loyalty to Local history and culture prompts his decision to depict the strike in this particular manner; in other words, if "we're all in it together," then working against Filipinos and Japanese was an obvious and regrettable mistake for Koreans. In light of the animosity between Koreans and Japanese, Sung Wha's sentiments in this case ring false. After all, Sung Wha is a patriot. Significantly, however, his objection to strikebreaking is largely *deracialized*. To him, the crime lies in the *principle* of strikebreaking because he understands the nature of worker exploitation:

> They work and sing while the sun—a swollen ball of fire—falls slowly on the not-so-distant sea. Cane is piled on a wagon, then loaded on flatbed railroad cars. Which take the harvest to the mill to be manufactured into raw sugar and bagasse. Then refined into white sugar.

> " . . . so dat da haole wahine housewife can make her tea party sweet someplace in da mainland someplace . . . so dat da kid who live down da block can lick his fav'rite lollipop . . . so dat da haole who own da plantation can make plenny mo' kālā on top da millions he already get. And he already living in dat big mansion up Nu'uanu Valley. And he get one nada big house on da North Shore, Mokulē'ia-side, and play polo wit' his stable of horses and wit' his rich friends who own da Big Island of Honolulu.[37]

However, Sung Wha's ambivalence over the situation manifests in his participation in strikebreaking, despite his guilty conscience. Although he maintains that "Japanese, Filipino, Korean . . . we're all the same" and that the real enemies are the "white bosses" (R 23), he cannot respond when another worker asks him why, if he objects so much, he works alongside the other Koreans in the fields during the strike. Clearly Sung Wha feels loyalty towards his Korean compatriots. Yet by focusing on the issue of capitalism, Sung Wha may uphold his Korean nationalist feelings at the same time he may display a fervent class consciousness.

Pak further asserts the complexity of Koreans' political positions in Hawai'i through Sung Wha's anti-American and anti-haole sentiments. Koreans wishing to ally themselves with the haole, in hopes that anti-Japanese sentiment will benefit them, find little in common with Sung Wha. Sung Wha refuses to play the role of the obedient worker and, knowing that his actions may cost him his life, confronts one particularly violent luna, thinking, *"Coward American, I'll cut you to pieces and leave you all over the field for the mongooses. That's what I'll do"* (R 22).[38] Class solidarity motivates Sung Wha here, yet does not interfere with his Korean nationalism. Rather, the other Korean workers liken him to Kim Chi Ha, another "radical" who eventually met with death because of his outspokenness. Such a comparison undeniably identifies Sung Wha as a patriot: the plantation bosses beat and banish Chi Ha because he is a "loud-mouth, radical Korean just off the boat spouting angry diatribes against the ruling plantation order, rousing the rest of those already hardheaded Koreans, turning them into an unmanageable, anarchistic mass" (R 34). Furthermore, Chi Ha is dismissed by the owners after they discover his anti-Japanese actions in Korea. The connection between Sung Wha and Chi Ha here thus fortifies Sung Wha's Korean nationalism. However, his fight ultimately remains against the oppressive order, whether it be Japanese or haole.

Unlike other Koreans who despise the Japanese in Hawai'i, Sung Wha recognizes Hawai'i as a territory *apart* from Korea. In Korea, the enemy is the Japanese government, whereas in Hawai'i, the plantation system becomes the root of exploitation:

> "Japanese are bastard pigs! Don't you know what they're doing to our country?

"The white bosses are bastard pigs!" (R 23)

Sung Wha perceives the distance between Korea and Hawai'i both physically and politically, yet this distance never allows him to forget the ways in which his life in Korea strongly informs his existence in the islands. Although he relegates Korea to the space of memory, these memories of Korea and Hawai'i commingle to form a landscape of longing and desire:

> The summer sun had reached its noonday height when he reached the Wahiawā Reservoir, and Kim Sung Wha, tired and hungry and shirtless and reddened from fire and sun, rested his sleepy and aching and dried eyes on the cool waters of a dark lake that . . . slowly fed itself through a complex of rivulets to the mighty Yalu River. And there, kneeling at the shore, he saw Hae Soon, facing the green mirror lake, her back toward him, sloughing her spring clothes that fell like large white feathers, washing her face and secret body parts. And far in the distance, almost completely hidden by clouds that perhaps held some snow, were the mountains. . . . And Sung Wha began to sing to himself as he looked down the gravelly road that would lead him to Wahiawā town, and he felt the breeze that smelled of eucalyptus and cane, and his eyes remembered the fields of cane that sloped gradually to the sea, their windblown tops moving in rhythmic, wavy patterns; and keeping time with them, he heard . . . drum beats bamboo slats against pigskin spiking damp crisp air, the song of return:

> *A-ri-rang, A-ri-rang,*
> *A-ra-ri-yo-o-o.*
> *A-ri-rang ko-gae-rul*
> *No-mo-gan-da.*[39] *(R 36)*

The folksong "Arirang" functions as a powerful indication of Sung Wha's identity as a patriot. Originally a song about two lovers separated by the Arirang Mountain, it later assumed political overtones as a death song for political prisoners and signified the separation of Koreans from their homeland.[40] Although Sung Wha continues as an activist for the disenfranchised in Hawai'i, memories of Korea never leave him, and the tenaciousness of his dream of returning indicates his unwillingness to compromise his ethnic identity within Local concerns. Sung Wha lacks the agency to return and in this sense takes part in a community of exiles. After losing money he has saved to Korean swindlers, he find comfort among Filipino workers who offer him sympathy and pineapple swipe to ease his troubles. Sung Wha's connection to them is not surprising, given the exilic nature of both Koreans' and Filipinos' journeys to Hawaiʻi.[41] In addition, their similar positions in the islands binds them, as he sees how "there is a lot in common, everyone being workers on the plantations owned by the haoles" (R 73). Despite their native language differences, he communicates comfortably with the Filipino workers through pidgin English—that is, until the conversation turns to the issue of capitalism and his opposition to the viewpoint that everyone wants to return home "with money to live like a king" (R 73). As Sung Wha insists that they must return home to fight the rich, pidgin becomes an increasingly inadequate vehicle for communication. Whereas pidgin has served as a symbol of Hawaii's historic multiethnic unity, in this particular scene it fails. Ironically, the language born of the working class cannot express counter-capitalist ideas. The rift between the speakers only heals through a reminder of their commonality; one worker's guitar literally silences Sung Wha's political rhetoric by evoking the pain and nostalgia of separation from the homeland:

> the singing commences: songs of lost love, of unrequited love, of love eternal, of fleeting love under the light of the moon. . . . How long, boys, how long, until our eyes can rest on beautiful Filipino women in their flowing sarongs and with the bright sunlight shimmering off their black-black hair held together in buns? (R 74)

Sung Wha later leaves the group with a strong sense of brotherhood and friendship, and we are told that although he knows no Ilocano, "he understands what his new friends are saying" (R 74). The juxtaposition of the inadequacy of pidgin with the communicability of Ilocano pinpoints the tension of Local cohesiveness: although "friendships and brotherhood [are] seamed together securely" (R 74), they are by no means seamless. The emphasis here lies on the shared experiences of Filipinos and Koreans, yet this commonality does not preclude differences owing to national affiliations. Although Eddie Miguel, a struggling cab driver, touchingly gives Sung Wha five dollars and a ride home after hearing of his dream of building a ricepaper airplane, Sung Wha's thoughts ultimately return to Korea and "his marvelous ricepaper airplane, flying in a clear blue sky" (R 78).

In his depiction of Sung Wha's later years, Pak questions the place of "living history" and Local activism in present-day Hawai'i. As an old man, Sung Wha comes to realize that generational differences begin to supersede racial ones as varying forms of Localness collide. Asked to speak to a class of University of Hawai'i students about his labor experiences, Sung Wha ventures into the city only to undergo a series of defamiliarizations. Although his audience consists of "local students, predominantly Orientals, a few pockets of Hawaiians and part-Hawaiians" (R 195), they have virtually no interest in Local history, Sung Wha, or his experiences. The university itself, which represents activism and rebellion in Sung Wha's ideals, instead houses apathetic students who regard him as invisible, diseased, and subhuman. Sung Wha confronts a new generation of Locals, born out of the labor experience in Hawai'i yet disconnected from it and its legacy; the Locals with whom Sung Wha is familiar in contrast appear old and irrelevant. Confined to memory as well as isolated pockets throughout the island, such as the run-down Kekaulike Hotel where Sung Wha lives, plantation Localism and its political aims fail to have meaning for the new Locals.

Even Sung Wha's own nephew, Yong Gil, cannot understand his uncle's fight to save Kekaulike Hotel from development into a modern office building: "'[T]he landlord, this is his place, he can do what he wants with it. The way you guys act, just like he owes you something. He doesn't owe you nothing'" (R 209). Ironically, Yong Gil sees Sung Wha's activism as destructive to his uncle's health, while Sung Wha's investment in Kekaulike is based upon his own sense of "survival": because his pride will not allow him to move in with Yong Gil, he must retain his room in the downtown hotel. Sung Wha secretly longs for a bed and good food under his nephew's care. Realizing that his old age prevents him from being the "radical" he once was, he feels that the *"young ones now, dey gotta take up the slack"* (R 212). He wishes to pass the torch on to the new generation, yet with the exception of Troy Nishimura, a teaching assistant, in addition to a few unnamed students, the prospects of this happening appear dismal indeed.

Politicized definitions of Localism call for a heritage originating in Hawaii's plantation experience. However, as Pak illustrates, heritage is not enough. Only direct historical connections can give meaning to the new generation of Locals. Yet if education provides the most ideal avenue for this to occur, what does it mean that the students at UH fail to recognize their ties to Sung Wha? Troy Nishimura seeks to establish connections between the students whose grandparents labored in Hawaii's agricultural industry and the "living history of labor in Hawai'i." But his attempts to bridge the gap between the two diverging Localisms in a classroom setting alienate him from both sides. The students remain bored, while Sung Wha wonders "why the hell was he invited to speak at the class in the first place" (R 195). In contrast, at Kekaulike Hotel, signs painted by some enthusiastic students bring comfort to Sung Wha, suggesting that the streets have supplanted the university as a site of resistance, in part because the university constructs a geography of privilege that erases Kekaulike from its map. The rift between "then" and "now" reflects the separation of the disenfranchised and the privileged. Affirming this, among the retired workers at the hotel are an equally rejected "handful of *mahus.*" Together, these men fight to preserve their claim to a "home" in the islands in ways the UH students cannot understand, ways that result from resignation and the realization of marginalized positions rather than self-righteousness:

> There were only expensive places to rent nowadays. You couldn't find a place for $130 a month, even though the place was fit enough only for rats and pigs and society's riffraff. What the hell . . . at least it was home for them; they could call this dump home. What the hell.
> (R 196)

The hotel, filled with "retirees from jobs and retirees from life," fosters the will to survive: the men, *"broken people with broken hearts and broken minds"* (R 205), hang on to their existences, their bodies material proof of Hawaii's past and present power relations.

Sung Wha remains in Hawai'i, yet his thoughts never leave Korea, his wife, or his children. His identity as a Local does not subsume his Korean identification even as he sees himself as part and parcel of Local history. As he comes to terms with his old age and failing body, his wish is to die in peace in Korea, indicating his sense of displacement:

Me . . . I one old horse now, jus' put me in da pasture. But funny,
yeah, dey no mo' one pasture fo' me ovah here. My pasture in Korea,
not here, even though I live most my life ovah here. Chee, but I still
no feel I belong. I wondah if evah going feel I belong. (R 212)

The source of this displacement comes less from an overt sense of
exclusion by other Locals in Hawai'i than Sung Wha's overwhelming
attachment to Korea. Like Pedro in Peter Hyun's *Man Sei!: The*
Making of a Korean American,[42] Sung Wha's experience in Korea
shapes his identity as a Korean American. By highlighting Sung Wha's
memories of Korea, *A Ricepaper Airplane*, like Margaret K. Pai's *The*
Dreams of Two Yi-Min and Ty Pak's *Guilt Payment*, attests to the link
between the global and the local. Sung Wha may have remained in
Hawai'i and become a part of its Local population, yet this does not
change the fact that political oppression brought him to the U.S.
against his will, thus challenging once more notions of nationhood and
Hawaii's "immigrant" population.

TWO POPULATIONS: THE LEGACY OF LOCAL KOREANS

Comparatively large numbers of post-1965 Korean immigrants in the
islands often lead many to mistakenly assume that Koreans have little
or no roots in plantation history, and it is this misconception with
which *A Ricepaper Airplane* takes issue. In writing Koreans into Local
history, Pak does not seek to eradicate Korean ethnicity in the name of
assimilation; the strong presence and persistence of Sung Wha's
memories of Korea in fact assert that "Local Koreans" have their own
specific ethnic and national narratives that seek to fill the gaps in
common perceptions of Local history.

Although Pak's latest work explores the dimensions of what we
call Local culture, it likewise exposes its weaknesses and failures, past
and present social divisions that belie a unified Local population whose
only threat may be the force of Hawaiian sovereignty. These ruptures
neither deny nor destroy the existence of Local sensibilities, only
illuminate a complex history that cannot be encapsulated in the concept
of paradise in the islands. In fact, Sung Wha stresses the need to "no
forget" to Yong Gil, precisely because he sees the danger in the "lucky
come Hawai'i"—and by extension, the "I like it here in America"—

ideology that threatens to delegitimize and invalidate very real struggles against the oppressive order in the U.S.:

> "No forget what I telling you, Yong Gil. Dis is history. Dis is what happened in da past. No forget all dis. Even when I *maké*, you remember what I telling you. No can forget how things was befo'. No make forget, like how da haoles trying make us forget everything what was like befo'. Dey trying brainwash everybody, tell us how us lucky live here, lucky come Hawai'i, lucky live in America, all dat bullshit. . . . Dem say how being one American is one big honor. . . . You dunno how much people wen suffer so much dose days jus' to make dem haoles rich and fat and get da high position dem get yesterday and today." (R 25-26)

In telling his story to Yong Gil, Sung Wha provides his nephew with a sense of his own roots in Korea, in addition to a Local history of resistance. As the two watch the sun set, Sung Wha transports Yong Gil to the plantations by telling him that "dis time of da day da best. Da plantation workers jus' coming home" (R 210). Their discussion eventually carries Yong Gil to Korea, where the sunset is "[m]o' beautiful dan Hawai'i" (R 211). Ultimately, Yong Gil declares, "'If you say the one in Korea is more beautiful than this one—and this one is beautiful—then I gotta see the one in Korea'" (R 211), signifying Yong Gil's acceptance of Sung Wha's gift: the legacy of his place in Local as well as Korean history.

NOTES

1. Robert Cazimero and Roland Cazimero, "Island in Your Eyes" on *The Best of the Brothers Cazimero, Vol. 2*, The Mountain Apple Company MAC-2011.
2. Roughly, "With love for my home in Kahalu'u." I thank Selena Loo and Michelle Akina for assisting me with this translation.
3. Sumida, *And the View From the Shore*, xiv-xv.
4. See Takaki, *Pau Hana.*
5. Trask, 249.
6. Darrell H. Y. Lum, introduction to *The Best of Bamboo Ridge*, ed. Eric Chock and Darrell H. Y. Lum (Honolulu: Bamboo Ridge Press, 1986), 3-5.

7. It is beyond the scope of this project to trace various racial transformations in native Hawaiian history. However, I would like to emphasize that racial definition for the kānaka maoli has a long and involved past, including a 1920 ruling by the U.S. Congress for the Hawaiian Homes Act stipulating that only those with 50% or more Hawaiian blood could qualify for the program. See *He Alo Ā He Alo.*

8. Michael Omi and Howard Winant, *Racial Formation in the United States From the 1960s to the 1990s,* 2nd ed. (New York: Routledge, 1994), 55. My italics.

9. "Foreign investment" and "Japanese investment" are all but synonymous in Hawai'i. Japanese purchases in 1990 constituted 98% of all foreign investment that year, and by the end of the year, was six times the amount of all other foreign investments combined. See James Mak and Marcia Y. Sakai, "Foreign Investment," *The Price of Paradise: Lucky We Live Hawaii?,* ed. Randall W. Roth (Honolulu: Mutual, 1992), 33-40.

10. While multinational corporations still headquarter themselves in a country of origin, transnational corporations "might no longer be tied to its nation of origin but is adrift and mobile, ready to settle anywhere and exploit any state including its own, as long as the affiliation serves its own interest." See Masao Miyoshi, "A Borderless World," *Critical Inquiry* 19 (Summer 1993): 726-751.

11. Rob Wilson and Arif Dirlik, introduction to *Asia/Pacific as Space of Cultural Production,* ed. Rob Wilson and Arif Dirlik (Durham: Duke University Press, 1995), 7-8.

12. For more on this, see Candace Fujikane, "Between Nationalisms: Hawaii's Local Nation and Its Troubled Paradise," *Critical Mass: A Journal of Asian American Cultural Criticism* 1.2 (Spring/Summer 1994): 23-57.

13. I make this statement self-consciously—many whites in the islands have complained of racial discrimination by Locals; however, it would be a mistake to categorize this discrimination as simply "anti-haole" without taking into consideration the long history of exploitation of people of color by haoles in Hawai'i, whether it be via whaling, sugar plantations, tourism, or the military. To a large degree, haoles have a long history as the "oppressors" in Hawai'i, and Local culture often builds its strength on its resistance to and exclusion of haoles for this very reason.

14. Dennis Kawaharada, "Images of Local Culture," *The Hawaii Herald,* 20 May 1983, 15.

15. Sumida, "Sense of Place," 215.

16. Gary Pak, *The Watcher of Waipuna and Other Stories* (Honolulu: Bamboo Ridge Press, 1992), 11. All subsequent quotes from this source will be indicated parenthetically with a "W" followed by a page number, e.g. (W 11).

17. Fujikane, 42.

18. The play is on the word "haole" here, which means "outsider" in Hawaiian. Although it has come to signify white people, it is hard to refute that Locals are likewise "outsiders" to Hawai'i.

19. This is not to condone homophobia, but to accentuate that the children have managed to move away from their parents' views. It is interesting to note that earlier in the story, the children admire Rosita's physique and view him as a role-model.

20. See Sumida, *And the View from the Shore.*

21. Sumida, "Sense of Place," 216.

22. Ali Behdad's notion of "belated travelers" calls attention to tourists' orientalist desires for a colonial past, one untainted by the bothersome subjectivities of the Other. Following this, if Hawai'i occupies a space in the cultural consciousness as a tropical get-away, then the erasure of Local and native histories and subjectivities becomes necessary. See Ali Behdad, *Belated Travelers: Orientalism in the Age of Colonial Dissolution* (Durham: Duke University Press, 1994).

23. For more on Japanese internment in Hawaii, see Okihiro, *Cane Fires,* chapters 9-11.

24. Sumida mentions that at the time of Pearl Harbor, there was an outbreak among Japanese on Kauai of inugami no sawarimono, or possession by a dog spirit. To curse one with an inugami, one must bury a dog up to its neck, then starve it. At the point of starvation, one places a piece of meat just out of the dog's reach, then beheads the dog. The head is then prayed to, to hunt out the victim. Sumida's allegorical reading of the possession involves America, during World War II, doing "the snatching and beheading in contracting the immigrants to labor in Hawai'i, starving them with promises of the future . . . then treating the immigrants as America's enemies and attempting to alienate the children not only from their parents but from their birthright of American citizenship." See Sumida, *And the View from the Shore,* 228.

25. Okihiro, *Cane Fires,* 121.

26. Although Gilbert's last name is Sanchez, Pak provides enough literary clues to inform us that Gilbert and his family are native Hawaiian.

27. Nakakura's "delusions" derive from his memories of World War II, and Gilbert's schizophrenia results from his losing his fiancée of eleven years to a haole GI.

28. For more on the impact of tourism and the military on Locals and Hawaiians, see Kent.

29. Rob Wilson, "Bloody Mary Meets Lois-Ann Yamanaka: Imagining Hawaiian Locality from *South Pacific* to Bamboo Ridge," *Public Culture* 8 (1995): 130-131.

30. As mentioned earlier, the appeal of this battle against outside investors for Local readers is that it allows the legitimization of Local land claims in ways that Hawaiian sovereignty does not.

31. In Hawaiian culture, Night Marchers are ghosts that walk the heights of mountains in rank. These ghosts are generally Hawaiian royalty, and it is punishable by death to look upon them. See Cunningham, 156.

32. Gary Pak, interview by author, 3 May 1994.

33. Okihiro, *Cane Fires*, 35.

34. Ibid., 18. Okihiro's failure to mention Korean plantation laborers is unfortunately characteristic of Korean erasure from plantation history, as is his minimal treatment of Korean-Japanese conflicts on the plantations.

35. Wong, 28-29.

36. Gary Pak, personal interview.

37. Gary Pak, *A Ricepaper Airplane* (Honolulu: University of Hawai'i Press, 1998), 24. Future material quoted from this source will be indicated parenthetically with an "R" followed by a page number, e.g. (R 24).

38. Souza is, presumably, of Portuguese descent. By positioning him as a "haole" and an "American," Pak calls attention to the hierarchical order of the plantations, in which many Portuguese (who are often considered Local) were employed to keep Hawaiian and Asian workers in line.

39. "Arirang, Arirang, I'm going over the Arirang hill." I thank Joyce Lee for this translation.

40. See Peter Hyun, *Man Sei!: The Making of a Korean American* (Honolulu: University of Hawai'i Press, 1986), 110.

41. The exilic link between Koreans and Filipinos is both historical and literary—like Korean American literature, Filipino American literature has remained largely "unmapped" and therefore misrepresented in the hierarchy of Asian American literature. See Oscar V. Campomanes, "Filipinos in the United States and Their Literature of Exile," in *Reading the Literatures of Asian America,* ed. Shirley Geok-lin Lim and Amy Ling (Philadelphia: Temple University Press, 1992), 49-78.

42. Hyun's work, though entitled *The Making of a Korean American*, takes place entirely in Asia and ends with Pedro's journey to America. This suggests that a Korean American is made in Korea, and that the colonial experience there plays a significant role in the immigration of Koreans to the U.S.

Epilogue

On a recent trip home to O'ahu, I stopped by Grace's Inn for my requisite plate lunch. Grace's boasts a variety of Local favorites, from teriyaki beef, to curry, to my favorite, chicken katsu. A plate lunch there includes an entree, two scoops of white rice, a scoop of macaroni salad, chow mein, and kimchee. As far back as I can remember, that little cup of kimchee always fascinated me. Somehow it was proof that I as a Korean had "made it" onto the Local plate. It was a small gesture, but an important one. A lot of times my friends would give away the cup of kimchee, either to me, or to the guys who didn't care if their breath smelled like garlic. Sometimes they asked to have it left off their lunches entirely. I never took this personally—after all, kimchee *does* smell.

In many ways, I accepted that scoop of kimchee as one of the few markers that said "Koreans were here" and, at the time, that was enough. But this last time home, when I went up to the counter to order my food, I noticed a new addition to the Grace's menu: meat jhun. Though I didn't order it (my mom makes the best jhun, anyway) I told this story to everyone I knew because the idea tickled me. Korean food had worked its way onto the list of Grace's specials.

While the Korean immigrant population has reinforced the perception of Koreans in the islands as FOBs, it has also compelled Local culture to take notice of its presence. There is little doubt in my mind that Grace's meat jhun has the recent immigrants to thank for its place on the menu. The newer Korean immigrants, because of their large numbers, have accomplished a visibility that the earlier immigrants could not. In a few generations, "Local" will unquestionably include "Korean," though politicized definitions of

"Local" will continue to demand a plantation history, which, as I have demonstrated in this dissertation, Koreans *do* have. Numbers are important. Early Korean plantation workers, unlike Japanese, Chinese, and Filipino laborers, did not have a large base, support network, and "contendability." Plantation labor practices, Korea's political situation, and U.S. policy shaped immigration conditions and consequently, Koreans' positions within Local culture.

If Koreans are working their way into Local culture, they must also confront their participation in a system that is *not* "post-colonial." My main focus here has not been Hawaiian sovereignty per se, yet I see the issues concerning Koreans in Local society as deeply tied to this discussion. Locals need to understand ruptures built into Local cultural and social politics as exemplified by the history of Koreans in Hawaiʻi. Locals also need to understand their role in the process of colonization, a practice that continues in the islands today. They must also understand what it is about Local culture's makeup that allows it to participate in the hegemonic practice. "Yellow guilt" cannot be of much use in this debate. It is not enough to say that we as Locals are as guilty as the haole, because this position fails to delineate how we as Locals are *different* from the haole. What Hawaiian sovereignty challenges us to do is to look at a more complex and "messy" system of colonization, not one that separates the island into two camps: oppressors and victims.

It would come as little surprise to those who know me that I have considerable emotional investment in the topic upon which I have chosen to write. This project has served as an avenue through which I can understand and politicize my own cultural identity. I remember that at certain moments of my childhood I felt embarrassed telling people I was Korean, in part because there seemed to be so few of us, but mostly because being Korean meant being "FOB" and in Hawaiʻi that meant "less." Admitting my ethnicity threatened to revoke my Local heritage. When I came to Los Angeles to attend college, those issues transformed into "Pan-Asian" ones, and for a long time I preferred to identify as "Asian American" in the same way I sought protection under the "Local" umbrella in Hawaiʻi. However, only after deciding to study Local and Korean American literature did I began to question Local culture, which, despite my childhood feelings of ethnic anxiety, I had seen as a multicultural ideal for so long, especially in contrast to my experiences with racism on the continent. Examining Local culture via

Korean writers from Hawai'i is entirely relevant not only for me, but perhaps for others who may have experienced a similar predicament.

Recently I returned home to be among the people who have always been my 'ohana, and having been surrounded by Locals once again, I realized that Hawai'i does have a "specialness" that is difficult to deny. Interrogating Localness is not a way to destroy it, but to understand my own place within in it, to come to terms with the feelings of exclusion I've sometimes had. What I plan to do through my work is to give voice to a "minority among the races" and to reclaim a history that until recently I did not see as my own.

Glossary

'āina:	land
AJA:	Americans of Japanese Ancestry; used by island Japanese to identify as "Japanese American"
ajumoni:	"auntie"; can refer to an elderly woman
ali'i:	Hawaiian royalty
aloha spirit:	a sense of generosity and giving inherited from traditional Hawaiian culture
banchan:	small side dishes served with a Korean meal
bar girls:	women who keep company with men in bars for money; not necessarily prostitutes
chicken katsu:	breaded, deep-fried chicken
ESS:	English Standard Schools; schools that required demonstration of "proficiency" in Standard English
FOB:	"Fresh Off the Boat"; a person born and raised in Asia
hahn:	Korean racially collective weariness and grief that comes from years of oppression
halmoni:	grandmother
hangul:	Korean language and writing

haole:	literally "foreigner"; commonly denotes a person of European descent
haole luna:	white foreman on the plantations
hapa:	literally "half"; at present, often refers to someone of Asian and European descent ("hapa haole")
harabuji:	grandfather
hauna:	a foul smell
hanbok:	Korean traditional dress for women
issei:	first generation Japanese in America
kahuna:	Hawaiian priest; usually though not exclusively from the ali'i class
kama'āina:	native-born
kanaka:	literally "person"; a Hawaiian (plural: kānaka)
kānaka maoli:	"the chosen people"; denotes indigenous people in Hawai'i
katonk:	a person of Asian descent born and raised on the continent
KB:	"Korean Bar" where bar girls work
kimchee:	spicy Korean pickles
koa:	a type of acacia tree
kye:	a system of rotating credit used by many Koreans
māhū:	homosexual
Mansei Rebellion:	the 1919 protest by Koreans against Japanese rule in Korea; thousands of unarmed Koreans were slaughtered
make:	die
meat jhun:	Korean dish of marinated meat that is floured, dipped in egg, then pan fried
nisei:	second generation Japanese in America

nohaku hānau:	sacred stones upon which ali'i women gave birth
'ohana:	family (not limited to blood relatives)
paniolo:	cowboy
picture brides:	women who came to Hawai'i and the U.S. to marry; these marriages were arranged by an exchange of pictures through a go-between
pidgin English:	creole language originating from the plantations; same as Hawai'i Creole English (HCE)
pupule:	crazy
sashimi:	raw fish
shaman:	in Korean culture, a woman healer whose methods originate from indigenous rituals
yangban:	an upperclass member of traditional Korean society
yi-min:	immigrants or settlers in a new land
yobo:	a Korean term of endearment; also means "Korean person" in Local slang

Bibliography

Abelmann, Nancy, and John Lie. *Blue Dreams: Korean Americans and the Los Angeles Riots.* Cambridge: Harvard University Press, 1995.

Act of War: The Overthrow of the Hawaiian Nation. Directed by Puhipau and Joan Lander. 58 min. Na Maka O Ka 'Āina, in association with the Center for Hawaiian Studies, University of Hawai'i at Mānoa, 1993. Videocassette.

Adams, Romanzo. *Interracial Marriage in Hawaii: A Study of the Mutually Conditioned Processes of Acculturation and Amalgamation.* New York: Macmillan, 1937.

Anderson, Benedict. *Imagined Communities: Reflections on the Origin and Spread of Nationalism.* New York: Verso, 1991.

Ashizawa, Becky. "Non-Hawaiian Role For a Nation Backed." *Honolulu Star-Bulletin,* 15 January 1993, A6.

Behdad, Ali. *Belated Travelers: Orientalism in the Age of Colonial Dissolution.* Durham: Duke University Press, 1994.

Blake, C. Fred. "Graffiti and Racial Insults: The Archaeology of Ethnic Relations in Hawaii." In *Modern Material Culture,* edited by Richard A. Gould and Michael B. Schiffer, 87-99. New York: Academic, 1981.

Brown, DeSoto, Anne Ellett, and Gary Giemza. *Hawaii Recalls: Selling Romance to America: Nostalgic Images of the Hawaiian Islands, 1910-1950.* Honolulu: Editions, 1982.

Burris, Jerry. "Islanders Support Hawaiian Cause." *Honolulu Advertiser,* 22 February 1994, A1, A4.

Campomanes, Oscar V. "Filipinos in the United States and Their Literature of Exile." *Reading the Literatures of Asian America,* edited by Shirley Geok-lin Lim and Amy Ling, 49-78. Philadelphia: Temple University Press, 1992.

Carr, Elizabeth Ball. *Da Kine Talk: From Pidgin to Standard English in Hawaii.* Honolulu: University of Hawai'i Press, 1972.

Cazimero, Robert and Roland Cazimero. "Island in Your Eyes." On *The Best of the Brothers Cazimero, Vol. 2.* The Mountain Apple Company, MAC-2011.

Cha, Kyung Soo. *Pumpkin Flower & Patriotism.* Los Angeles: Korean American Educational Research Center, 1991.

Cha, Theresa. *Dictee.* New York: Tanam, 1982.

Chai, Alice. "A Picture Bride from Korea: The Life History of a Korean American Woman in Hawaii." *Bridge: An Asian American Perspective* (1979): 1-12.

Chang, Curtis. "Streets of Gold: The Myth of the Model Minority." In *Rereading America*, edited by Gary Columbo, Robert Cullen, and Bonnie Lisle, 54-64. Boston: Bedford, 1992.

Chang, Roberta, Robin Lee, and Hong Yul Kim. *We Want to Be Americans.* Translated by Dong Jae Lee. Honolulu: General Assistance Center for the Pacific, College of Education, University of Hawai'i, 1975.

Chesney-Lind, Meda, and Ian Y. Lind. "Visitors as Victims: Crimes Against Tourists in Hawaii." *Annals of Tourism Research* 13 (1986): 167-191.

Chin, Frank, et al., eds. *Aiiieeeee!: An Anthology of Asian-American Writers.* Washington, D.C.: Howard University Press, 1983.

Cho, Sumi K. "Korean American vs. African American: Conflict and Construction." In *Reading Rodney King/Reading Urban Uprising*, edited by Robert Gooding-Williams, 196-211. New York: Routledge, 1993.

Chock, Eric, and Darrell H.Y. Lum, eds. *The Best of Bamboo Ridge Quarterly.* Honolulu: Bamboo Ridge Press, 1986.

Chock, Eric, et al., eds. *Talk Story: An Anthology of Hawaii's Local Writers.* Honolulu: Petronium/Talk Story, 1978.

Ch'oe, Yong-ho. "The Early Korean Immigrants to Hawaii: A Background History." In *Korean Immigrants in Hawaii: A Symposium on Their Background History, Acculturation and Public Policy Issues*, edited by Myongsup Shin and Daniel B. Lee, 1-17. Honolulu: Korean Immigrant Welfare Association of Hawaii and Operation Manong, College of Education, University of Hawai'i, 1978.

Choi, Sook Nyul. *Year of Impossible Goodbyes.* Boston: Houghton Mifflin, 1991.

Cooper, George, and Gavan Daws. *Land and Power in Hawaii.* Honolulu: University of Hawai'i Press, 1985.

Cumings, Bruce. *The Origins of the Korean War Vol. 1: Liberation and the Emergence of Separate Regimes 1945-1947.* Princeton: Princeton University Press, 1981.

Cunningham, Scott. *Hawaiian Religion & Magic.* St. Paul, MN: Llewellyn, 1995.

Day, A. Grove, and Karl Stevens, eds. *The Hawaiian Reader.* New York: Appleton Century-Crofts, 1959.

DeLima, Frank. Interview by Jeff Chang, Darcie Iki, and Darlene Rodrigues. 12 November 1994.

Du Puy, William Atherton. *Hawaii and Its Race Problem.* Washington, D.C.: U.S. Government Printing Office, 1932.

During, Simon. "Postmodernism or Post-colonialism Today." *Textual Practice* 1.1 (1987): 12-47.

Espiritu, Yen Le. *Asian American Panethnicity: Bridging Institutions and Identities.* Philadelphia: Temple University Press, 1992.

Fujikane, Candace. "Between Nationalisms: Hawaii's Local Nation and Its Troubled Paradise." *Critical Mass: A Journal of Asian American Cultural Criticism* 1.2 (Spring/Summer 1994): 23-57.

Furrer, Roger MacPherson, ed. *He Alo Ā He Alo: Hawaiian Voices on Sovereignty.* Honolulu: The Hawaii Area Office of the American Friends Service Committee, 1993.

Goulden, Joseph C. *Korea: The Untold Story of the War.* New York: McGraw-Hill, 1982.

Grant, Glen, and Dennis M. Ogawa. "Living Proof: Is Hawaii the Answer?" *ANNALS, AAPSS* 530 (November 1993): 137-154.

Hara, Marie. "Fourth Grade Ukus." *Bamboo Ridge* 47 (Summer 1990): 88-98.

Harvey, Young Sook Kim, and Soon-Hyung Chung. "The Koreans." In *People and Cultures of Hawaii: A Psychocultural Profile,* edited by John F. McDermott, Jr., Wen-Shing Tseng, and Thomas W. Maretzki, 135-154. Honolulu: John A. Burns School of Medicine and the University of Hawai'i Press, 1980.

History. Korea Background Series. Seoul, Korea: Korea Overseas Information Service, 1978.

Hyun, Peter. *Man Sei!: The Making of a Korean American.* Honolulu: University of Hawai'i Press, 1986.

Kamau'u, Mahealani, and H.K. Bruss Keppler. "'What Might Sovereignty Look Like?'" In *The Price of Paradise, Volume II,* edited by Randall W. Roth, 295-301. Honolulu: Mutual, 1993.

Kang, K. Connie. *Home Was the Land of Morning Calm: A Saga of a Korean-American Family.* Reading, MA: Addison-Wesley, 1995.

Kang, Younghill. *The Grass Roof.* New York: Scribner, 1934.

Kawaharada, Dennis. "Images of Local Culture." *The Hawaii Herald,* 20 May 1983, 1, 11, 15.

Kent, Noel J. *Hawaii: Islands Under the Influence.* Honolulu: University of Hawai'i Press, 1983.

Kido, Pamela Sachi. "Local Identity in a (Trans)Nationalist Hawaiian Space." *The Office for Womens' Research Student Working Papers Series* 1 (1995): 22-24.

Kim, Bernice. "The Koreans in Hawaii." Master's Thesis, University of Hawai'i, 1937.

Kim, Elaine H. "Home is Where the *Han* Is: A Korean American Perspective on the Los Angeles Upheavals." *Reading Rodney King/Reading Urban Uprising,* edited by Robert Gooding-Williams, 215-235. New York: Routledge, 1993.

———. "Korean American Literature." *An Interethnic Companion to Asian American Literature,* edited by King-Kok Cheung, 156-191. New York: Cambridge University Press, 1997.

Kim, Jung Ki. "Some Value Questions for Ethnic Orientation: An Ethical Perspective on Korean Immigration Motives." In *Korean Immigrants in Hawaii: A Symposium on Their Background History, Acculturation and Public Policy Issues,* edited by Myongsup Shin and Daniel B. Lee, 18-26. Honolulu: Korean Immigrant Welfare Association of Hawaii and Operation Manong, College of Education, University of Hawai'i, 1978.

Kim Ronyong. *Clay Walls.* Seattle: University of Washington Press, 1987.

Kim Yong Ik. "Translation President." *Hudson Review* 33.2 (1980): 233-244.

Ko, Seung K. "Korean Immigrants' Political Orientation and Problems of Political Socialization." In *Korean Immigrants in Hawaii: A Symposium on Their Background History, Acculturation and Public Policy Issues,* edited by Myongsup Shin and Daniel B. Lee, 36-43. Honolulu: Korean Immigrant Welfare Association of Hawaii and Operation Manong, College of Education, University of Hawai'i, 1978.

Kosasa-Terry, Geraldine. "Diasporic Spaces: Rethinking Sites of Immigration/Countering the Narrative of a Nation." Paper presented at the "Configuring Pacific Diasporas: Indigenous and Immigrant

Communities" conference sponsored by the Association of Asian American Studies, Honolulu, 26 March 1996.

Laney, Leroy O. "'Why Is the Cost of Living in Hawaii So High? Will It Ever Come Down?'" In *The Price of Paradise: Lucky We Live Hawaii?*, edited by Randall W. Roth, 23-31. Honolulu: Mutual, 1992.

Lee, Chang-rae. *Native Speaker.* New York: Riverhead, 1995.

Lee, Ki-baik. *A New History of Korea.* Translated by Edward W. Wagner and Edward J. Schultz. Cambridge: Harvard University Press, 1984.

Lee, Marie G. *Finding My Voice.* Boston: Houghton Mifflin, 1992.

———. *If It Hadn't Been for Yoon Jun.* Boston: Houghton Mifflin, 1993.

Lee, Mary Paik. *Quiet Odyssey: A Pioneer Korean Woman in America*, edited by Sucheng Chan. Seattle: University of Washington Press, 1990.

Lee, Samuel S. O., ed. *50 Years of St. Luke's Church.* Honolulu: Paradise of the Pacific, 1957.

———. *Their Footsteps: A Pictorial History of Koreans in Hawaii Since 1903.* Honolulu: The Committee on the 90th Anniversary Celebration of Korean Immigration to Hawaii, 1993.

Lew, Walter. *Excerpts From Dikte for Dictee.* Seoul: Yeul Eum, 1992.

Lim, Shirley Geok-lin. "Assaying the Gold: Or, Contesting the Ground of Asian American Literature." *New Literary History* 24 (1993): 147-169.

———. "Immigration and Diaspora." In *An Interethnic Companion to Asian American Literature*, edited by King-Kok Cheung, 289-311. New York: Cambridge University Press, 1997.

Lowe, Lisa. "Heterogeneity, Hybridity, Multiplicity: Marking Asian American Differences." *Diaspora* (Spring 1991): 23-44.

Lum, Wing Tek. *Expounding the Doubtful Points.* Honolulu: Bamboo Ridge Press, 1987.

Mak, James, and Marcia Y. Sakai. "Foreign Investment." In *The Price of Paradise: Lucky We Live Hawaii?*, edited by Randall W. Roth, 33-40. Honolulu: Mutual, 1992.

Makino, Valerie. "Non-Hawaiians Are Worried." *Honolulu Advertiser*, 12 July 1994, A6.

McCune, Shannon. *The Mansei Movement.* Honolulu: The Center for Korean Studies, University of Hawai'i, 1976.

Miyoshi, Masao. "A Borderless World." *Critical Inquiry* 19 (Summer 1993): 726-751.

Montrose, Louis Adrian. "A Midsummer Night's Dream and the Shaping Fantasies of Elizabethan Culture: Gender, Power, Form." In *Rewriting the Renaissance*, edited by Margaret W. Ferguson, Maureen Quilligan, and Nancy J. Vickers, 65-87. Chicago: Chicago University Press, 1986.

Morgan, William Michael. "The Anti-Japanese Origins of the Hawaiian Annexation Treaty of 1987." *Diplomatic History* 6.1 (1982): 23-44.

Morson, Gary Saul, and Caryl Emerson. *Mikhail Bakhtin: Creation of a Prosaics.* Stanford: Stanford University Press, 1990.

Okamura, Jonathan Y. "Aloha Kanaka Me Ke Aloha 'Āina: Local Culture and Society in Hawaii." *Amerasia* 7.2 (1980): 119-137.

———. "The Illusion of Paradise: Multiculturalism in Hawai'i." Paper presented at the "Reconfiguring Minority-Majority Discourse: Problematizing Multiculturalism Programs in Cultural Studies" conference sponsored by the University of Hawai'i East-West Center, Honolulu, August 1994.

———. "The Jangled Discourse of Race Relations in Hawai'i." Paper presented at the "Configuring Pacific Diasporas: Indigenous and Immigrant Communities" conference sponsored by the Association of Asian American Studies, Honolulu, 26 March 1996.

———. "Why There Are No Asian Americans in Hawai'i: The Continuing Significance of Local Identity." *Social Process in Hawaii* 35 (1994): 161-178.

Okihiro, Gary. *Cane Fires: The Anti-Japanese Movement in Hawaii, 1865-1945.* Philadelphia: Temple University Press, 1991.

———. "The Picnic." *Japanese American National Museum Quarterly* 10.2 (1995): 4-11.

Omi, Michael, and Howard Winant. *Racial Formation in the United States From the 1960s to the 1990s.* 2nd ed. New York: Routledge, 1994.

Pai, Margaret K. *The Dreams of Two Yi-Min.* Honolulu: University of Hawai'i Press, 1989.

Pak, Gary. *A Ricepaper Airplane.* Honolulu: University of Hawai'i Press, 1998.

———. "Catching a Big Ulua." *Bamboo Ridge* 47 (Summer 1990): 17-27.

———. "Excerpt from *Children of a Fire Land.*" *Bamboo Ridge* 47 (Summer 1990): 28-41.

———. Personal interview by author. 3 May 1994.

———. *The Watcher of Waipuna and Other Stories.* Honolulu: Bamboo Ridge Press, 1992.

Pak, Ty. *Guilt Payment.* Honolulu: Bamboo Ridge Press, 1983.

———. "The Tiger Cub." *Amerasia Journal* 18.3 (1992): 51-60.

Palumbo-Liu, David. "Universalisms and Minority Culture." *differences: A Journal of Feminist Cultural Studies* 7.1 (1995): 188-208.

Parker, Linda S. "Federal Management of Native Hawaiians." *Journal of the West* 15.2 (April 1976): 92-101.

Patterson, Wayne. *The Korean Frontier in America: Immigration to Hawaii 1896-1910.* Honolulu: University of Hawai'i Press, 1988.

Perkins, Leialoha A. "Hawaiians in Hawai'i Literature and Publishing." Paper presented at the "Configuring Pacific Diasporas: Indigenous and Immigrant Communities" conference sponsored by the Association of Asian American Studies. Honolulu, 26 March 1996.

Peterson, Jonathan. "Honolulu Sets Pattern as Capital of Diversity." *Los Angeles Times,* 10 January 1994, A1, A12, A14.

Philion, Stephen. "Hawai'i: Multiethnic Haven? Mythology and History." Paper presented at the "Configuring Pacific Diasporas: Indigenous and Immigrant Communities" conference sponsored by the Association of Asian American Studies. Honolulu, 25 March 1996.

Pratt, Mary Louise. *Imperial Eyes: Travel Writing and Transculturation.* New York: Routledge, 1992.

Pukui, Mary Kawena, and Caroline Curtis. *The Water of Kane.* Honolulu: Kamehameha Schools Press, 1951.

Pukui, Mary Kawena, and Samuel H. Elbert. *Hawaiian Dictionary: Hawaiian-English, English-Hawaiian.* Honolulu: University of Hawai'i Press, 1986.

Rosa, John Chock. "'Local' in the Thirties: The Massie Case and Hawaii's Asian Pacific Americans." Paper presented at the "Configuring Pacific Diasporas: Indigenous and Immigrant Communities" conference sponsored by the Association of Asian American Studies. Honolulu, 26 March 1996.

Rosegg, Peter. "Majority Is Against Hawaiian Land Return." *Honolulu Advertiser,* 4 August 1994, A1, A2.

Roth, Randall W. *The Price of Paradise: Lucky We Live Hawaii?* Honolulu: Mutual, 1992.

———. *The Price of Paradise, Volume II.* Honolulu: Mutual, 1993.

Said, Edward W. *Orientalism.* New York: Vintage, 1978.

Sanders, Daniel S. "Social Policies and Welfare Issues in Relation to Korean Immigrants." In *Korean Immigrants in Hawaii: A Symposium on Their Background History, Acculturation and Public Policy Issues,* edited by Myongsup Shin and Daniel B. Lee, 27-35. Honolulu: Korean

Immigrant Welfare Association of Hawaii and Operation Manong, College of Education, University of Hawai'i, 1978.

Shirota, Jon. *Lucky Come Hawaii.* Honolulu: Bess Press, 1988.

Smith, William C. "The Hybrid in Hawaii as a Marginal Man." *American Journal of Sociology* 39.4 (January 1934): 459-468.

Soja, Edward W. *Postmodern Geographies: The Reassertion of Space in Critical Social Theory.* New York: Verso, 1989.

Sollors, Werner, ed. *The Invention of Ethnicity.* New York: Oxford University Press, 1989.

Song, Cathy. *Frameless Windows, Squares of Light.* New York: Norton, 1988.

———. *Picture Bride.* New Haven: Yale University Press, 1983.

———. *School Figures.* Pittsburgh: University of Pittsburgh Press, 1994.

Stewart, Frank, ed. *Passages to the Dream Shore.* Honolulu: University of Hawai'i Press, 1987.

Sumida, Stephen H. *And the View from the Shore: Literary Traditions of Hawai'i.* Washington: University of Washington Press, 1991.

———. "Postcolonialism, Nationalism, and the Emergence of Asian/Pacific American Literatures." In *An Interethnic Companion to Asian American Literature,* edited by King-Kok Cheung, 274-288. New York: Cambridge University Press, 1997.

———. "Sense of Place, History, and the Concept of the 'Local' in Hawaii's Asian/Pacific American Literatures." In *Reading the Literature of Asian America,* edited by Shirley Geok-lin Lim and Amy Ling, 215-238. Philadelphia: Temple University Press, 1992.

Sur, Wilma. "Korean Ethnic Nationalism." *Hawaii Pono Journal* Fourth Quarter (1970): 17-31.

Takaki, Ronald. *Pau Hana: Plantation Life and Labor in Hawaii.* Honolulu: University of Hawai'i Press, 1983.

———. *Strangers From a Different Shore.* New York: Penguin, 1989.

Thompson, David E. "The ILWU as a Force for Interracial Unity in Hawaii." In *Kodomo No Tame Ni: The Japanese American Experience in Hawaii,* edited by Dennis M. Ogawa and Glen Grant, 486-512. Honolulu: University of Hawai'i Press, 1978.

Trask, Haunani-Kay. *From a Native Daughter: Colonialism and Sovereignty in Hawai'i.* Monroe, ME: Common Courage, 1993.

———. *Light in the Crevice Never Seen.* Corvallis, OR: Calyx, 1994.

Trimillo, Ricardo J. Panel discussion at the "Strategizing Cultures" conference sponsored by the University of Caifornia at Los Angeles, Spring 1993.

Troubled Paradise. Directed by Steven Okazaki. 58 min. National Asian American Telecommunications Association and Farallon Films, 1992. Videocassette.

Vinacke, W. Edgar. "Stereotyping Among National-Racial Groups in Hawaii: A Study in Ethnocentrism." *The Journal of Social Psychology* 30 (1949): 265-291.

Walsh, Joan. "Asian Women, Caucasian Men." *Image,* 2 December 1990, 11-16.

Watanabe, Sylvia, and Carol Bruchac, eds. *Home to Stay: Asian American Women's Fiction.* Greenfield Center, NY: Greenfield Review, 1990.

Watson, Sophie, and Katherine Gibson, eds. *Postmodern Cities & Spaces.* Cambridge: Blackwell, 1995.

Whittaker, Elvi. *The Mainland HAOLE: The White Experience in Hawaii.* New York: Columbia University Press, 1986.

Wilson, Rob. "Bloody Mary Meets Lois-Ann Yamanaka: Imagining Hawaiian Locality from *South Pacific* to Bamboo Ridge." *Public Culture* 8 (1995): 127-158.

———. "Goodbye Paradise: Global/Localism, Hawaii, and Cultural Production in the American Pacific." *New Formations* 24 (Winter 1994): 35-50.

Wilson, Rob, and Arif Dirlik, eds. *Asia/Pacific as Space of Cultural Production.* Durham: Duke University Press, 1995.

Wong, Saul-ling Cynthia. *Reading Asian American Literature: From Necessity to Extravagance.* Princeton: Princeton University Press, 1993.

Yamada, Joanne Y. "Excerpt from *Shizue's World.*" *Bamboo Ridge* 24 (Winter 1985): 38-63.

Yamamoto, Eric. "From 'Japanee' to Local: Community Change and the Redefinition of Sansei Identity in Hawaii." Master's Thesis, University of Hawai'i, 1974.

Yamanaka, Lois Ann. *Saturday Night at the Pahala Theatre.* Honolulu: Bamboo Ridge Press, 1993.

Yang, Sarah Lee. "Koreans in Hawai'i." *Social Process in Hawaii* 29 (1982): 89-94.

Index

'A'ala Park, 10, 19
'āina. *See* land
African American, 88-89, 98
AJA, 72, 103
  See also Japanese
Ala Moana, 8, 19
ali'i, 105, 106
aloha spirit, as commodity, 7
American Dream, 15, 27, 82, 84
  as economic mobility, 31-32,
    33, 44, 80
  constructing gender, 41-43, 89
  myth of, 28, 29, 30-31, 38, 52,
    53, 54
  promising new beginning, 71,
    74
Americanization Programs, 47
Americanness, 16, 61, 72, 76, 77,
  79, 90, 91, 118
  and Local identity, 12, 14, 15,
    75
  as representation of power, 4,
    15, 34, 41, 45, 50, 51, 69,
    80, 85, 124
  as salvation, 68, 69, 70
  based on whiteness, 12
  constraint of, 68

influence on Korean
  Nationalism, 15
relationship to Asian American,
  12
reliant upon Korea, 81
Arirang, 119
Asian American, 97
  challenges to, 74
  culture, 5
  identity, 11-12
  vs. Local identity, 11
  literature compared with Local
    literature, 4

Brady Bunch, The, 3
Bulosan, Carlos, 12

Chan, Jeffrey Paul, 11
Chin, Frank, 11
Chinese, 46, 47, 50, 51
  at Schofield Barracks, 37
  on plantations, 26, 27, 114
  women, 87
Chinese Exclusion Act of 1882, 26
Christianity, 86
  enabling Korean Nationalism,
    27, 33-34, 73

147

class structure, 105-106
dispossession, 35-36, 37, 74,
    105, 106
historical sites, 3
    selling of, 9
    trespassing upon, 4
homeless population, 19
land struggle, 16
on plantations, 114
rights, 112
strikebreakers, 13
"Hawaiian at heart," 6, 101
Hawaiian Homes Act, 125
Hawaiian Nation, colonization of,
    106
    overthrow of, 35
Hawaiian sovereignty, 19, 37,
    100, 102
    affecting Local identity, 5, 6, 8,
    35-36, 74, 99, 101, 123
homosexuality, 106, 107, 122
Hong Kong, 53
Hyun, Peter, 123

Illocano, 120
immigrants, 4, 51, 91, 102
    perceived as FOBs, 5
    post-1965, 5, 13, 16
    women, sexual commodification
    of, 87
immigration, 81,
    affecting class status, 15, 30-34
    as a result of conspiratorial
    factors, 30, 34, 35, 90, 123
Institute for the Advancement of
    Hawaiian Affairs, 6
International Longshoremen's and
    Warehousemen's Union
    (ILWU), 14

Japanese, 46, 50, 75, 84, 85, 9,
    111
    at Schofield Barracks, 37
    colonization, 12, 26, 38, 63,
    116, 118
    effect on Koreans in Hawai'i,
    8, 13, 14, 24, 27, 34, 36, 60-
    61, 70-71, 75
    giving rise to Korean
    emigration, 26
    espionage theories during WWII,
    111
    influence in Hawaii's economy,
    4, 47, 103
    internment of, 4, 111
    nationals and investment, 101,
    108
    on plantations, 26, 27, 113,
    114, 117, 118
    women, 87
    WWII surrender of, 62

Ka Lāhui Hawai'i, 6
kahuna, 98, 103, 105
kānaka maoli. *See* Hawaiian
katonks, 12
Kamehameha I, 9
Ke'eaumoku, 5, 23
Kewalo Basin, 10
Kim, Bernice, 37
Kim, Elaine, 81
Kim Ronyoung, 30
Korea, 81, 118, 119, 121
    attachment to by Koreans, 66,
    70, 73, 116, 119-120, 122-
    123, 124
    civil opposition within, 63

connection to American and
Local identity, 91
Korean American, identity, 64, 68,
70, 71, 79
Korean bar girls, 23, 81, 85, 86-
87, 93, 103
Korean Bars (KBs), 81, 86, 87
proliferation of, 5, 103
Korean Nationalism, 12, 26, 31,
54, 78, 116, 118
affected by notions of
Americanness, 15
and gender roles, 16, 33, 41-43
in Hawai'i, 33, 38, 72, 73
Korean women's participation
in, 33, 44-45
Local culture's relationship to,
15, 16, 36
role of Christianity within, 27,
33-34, 73
shaped by class status, 33
Korean War, 60, 62-65, 69, 70, 71,
72, 76
affecting Koreans in Hawai'i, 61
Koreans, 47
affected by Japanese
colonization, 8, 13, 14, 24,
26, 27, 34, 36, 60-61, 70-71,
75
against Japanese in Hawai'i, 8,
14, 36, 37-38, 43, 44, 71,
117, 118
as cheap labor, 80
See also plantations, laborers
on, and plantations, owners
seeking labor
desire for assimilation into haole
society, 36, 47, 71-72, 118

economic success of in Hawai'i,
38
exile, 14, 16, 72, 73, 74, 75,
92, 120
generational divisions among,
66
identity, 61, 72, 75, 77, 78, 79,
85, 122
immigrants, 26, 52, 54, 60, 71,
72, 75, 86, 116
first group of, 4, 13, 26
post-1965, 9, 16, 64-66, 90-
91, 123
difficulties faced by, 64-65
marginalization of, 8, 9, 12, 14,
16, 17, 24, 60, 65, 66, 82,
87, 91, 96, 116, 123
Methodists, 52
misrepresentation in history,
13, 14
nationality, 84, 87, 89
position of gender within, 81,
82, 83, 85
on plantations, 24, 27, 31-32,
37, 96, 116, 117, 123, 124
outmarriage in Hawai'i, 8, 65
perceived as "new arrivals" to
U.S., 91, 95-96
position in islands, 4
racial separatism in Hawai'i, 46,
51, 65
reaction to Mansei Rebellion,
14, 36, 117
shamans, 82-84,
strikebreakers, 13, 14, 36, 117,
118
vs. Local society, 5, 36, 51, 61,
65

For Product Safety Concerns and Information please contact our EU
representative GPSR@taylorandfrancis.com
Taylor & Francis Verlag GmbH, Kaufingerstraße 24, 80331 München, Germany

9 781138 964594